D0179588

formatio

TRADITION. EXPERIENCE.
TRANSFORMATION.

Formatio books from InterVarsity Press follow the rich tradition of the church in the journey of spiritual formation. These books are not merely about being informed, but about being transformed by Christ and conformed to his image. Formatio stands in InterVarsity Press's evangelical publishing tradition by integrating God's Word with spiritual practice and by prompting readers to move from inward change to outward witness. InterVarsity Press uses the chambered nautilus for Formatio, a symbol of spiritual formation because of its continual spiral journey outward as it moves from its center. We believe that each of us is made with a deep desire to be in God's presence. Formatio books help us to fulfill our deepest desires and to become our true selves in light of God's grace.

hodes, Tricia McCary.
acred chaos :
piritual disciplines fo
2008.
3305216217244
h   08/29/08

WITHDRAWN

Tricia McCary Rhodes

FOREWORD BY Gary Thomas

S A C R E D
C H A O S

Spiritual Disciplines for the Life You Have

IVP Books

An imprint of InterVarsity Press
Downers Grove, Illinois

InterVarsity Press
P.O. Box 1400, Downers Grove, IL 60515-1426
World Wide Web: www.ivpress.com
E-mail: email@ivpress.com

©2008 by Tricia McCary Rhodes

All rights reserved. No part of this book may be reproduced in any form without written permission from InterVarsity Press.

InterVarsity Press® is the book-publishing division of InterVarsity Christian Fellowship/USA®, a student movement active on campus at hundreds of universities, colleges and schools of nursing in the United States of America, and a member movement of the International Fellowship of Evangelical Students. For information about local and regional activities, write Public Relations Dept., InterVarsity Christian Fellowship/USA, 6400 Schroeder Rd., P.O. Box 7895, Madison, WI 53707-7895, or visit the IVCF website at <www.intervarsity.org>.

All Scripture quotations, unless otherwise indicated, are taken from the New American Standard Bible®, *copyright 1960, 1962, 1963, 1968, 1971, 1972, 1973, 1975, 1977, 1995 by The Lockman Foundation. Used by permission.*

Design: Cindy Kiple
Images: iStockphoto

ISBN 978-0-8308-3512-6

Printed in the United States of America ∞

g green press INITIATIVE *InterVarsity Press is committed to protecting the environment and to the responsible use of natural resources. As a member of the Green Press Initiative we use recycled paper whenever possible. To learn more about the Green Press Initiative, visit <www.greenpressinitiative.org>.*

Library of Congress Cataloging-in-Publication Data

Rhodes, Tricia McCary.
 Sacred chaos: spiritual disciplines for the life you have / Tricia McCary Rhodes.
  p. cm.
 Includes bibliographical references.
 ISBN 978-0-8308-3512-6 (pbk.: alk. paper)
 1. Spiritual life—Christianity. I. Title.
 BV4501.3.R46 2008
 248.4'6—dc22

                                                                                    2008005934

P	19	18	17	16	15	14	13	12	11	10	9	8	7	6	5	4	3	2	1
Y	24	23	22	21	20	19	18	17	16	15	14	13	12	11	10	09	08			

To my grandchildren,

Marni and Abe,

whose presence has helped me discover

the sacred within the chaos of the life I have

Contents

Foreword

What will *really* help you grow more: going off on a solitary retreat, Bible in tow, and fasting for an entire weekend, or taking a long road trip in a minivan with three small children and an occasionally grumpy spouse? Which experience do you think will truly call out your pride and invite you to live a life of service, forgiveness and gentleness?

Even hermits recognized the soul-scouring benefits of vocational and family life. Theophan the Recluse taught that the hermetic life is less well-suited to address certain spiritual failings: "Life lived in common with others is more suitable," he said, "because it provides us with practical experience in struggling with the passions and overcoming them. In solitude, the struggle goes on only in the mind, and is often as weak in its effect as the impact of a fly's wing."

This isn't to deny the value of occasional retreat-taking, and certainly not to cast doubt on the value of solitude; both are well-known prescriptions for spiritual growth. But Christians need to reclaim the value of embracing the occasional chaos of family and vocational life—life in the real world—for the spiritual benefits that they present us with every day (and often, almost by the minute).

Tricia Rhodes's own life experience as a wife, mother, grandmother, author, speaker and earnest believer provides a deep well of drama and wisdom, out of which she challenges us to embrace the occasional chaos of real life and learn to see, meet with and worship God in the midst of it. I can't imagine a better aim or a more pleasant guide than Tricia as she takes us on this fascinating and rich journey.

I have long been a fan of Tricia Rhodes's writing, but *Sacred Chaos* is her best work yet, her tour de force of real-life spirituality. It is immensely practical, while grappling seriously with the demands of everyday life. It is chock full of arresting images; Tricia makes spiritual truth seem very vivid yet also very reachable. She has mastered the art of making the mundane serve the cause of the marvelous and even the miraculous.

Your life *can* find room for a growing and rich relationship with God; this book will show you how.

Gary Thomas

Acknowledgments

I am full of gratitude to many who have been in the trenches with me throughout the process of writing this book. I am constantly amazed at a God who chooses to use me in spite of myself and fills me with joy along the way. All praise and honor to his name!

Thanks to Cindy Bunch and the team at InterVarsity Press for having a vision and helping me to craft the message. You understood what this book was meant to be when I wasn't sure. It is a privilege to work with such quality people. Your integrity and spiritual focus inspire me.

Thanks to my agent and friend Steve Laube, who has continually challenged me to go the distance, believing in God's call on my life when I doubted it myself. Your constant support and timely wisdom mean so much to me.

My deepest appreciation and thanks to Joe, my husband, pastor, resident theologian and spiritual mentor, who has listened, advised, edited, questioned and cheered me on for more than three decades now. I couldn't do it without you.

For more resources on your spiritual journey, see my website: <www.soulatrest.com>. And if you'd like more information, feel free to e-mail me at tricia@soulatrest.com.

Introduction

It wasn't supposed to be this way.

This was supposed to be a book about sacred space, about ways you and I can increase our intimacy with God by embracing various spiritual disciplines. Enamored with the possibilities of things like personal retreats, contemplative walks along the beach, withdrawal from the chaos of life and seasons of silence and solitude, I couldn't wait to write the thing.

The only problem was that there didn't seem to be any space at all, sacred or otherwise, in my life. There was the ordinary minutia—things like paying the bills and answering e-mails and fixing broken dryers and trimming the bushes and shopping for groceries and returning phone calls, to name a few. There were articles to write and people to care for and ministries to perform and community activities to pursue and relationships to maintain at home with my husband and almost grown child. Then— and I can almost see the smile on God's face at this one—our oldest son, his wife and our two grandchildren moved in with us for a season. Not only did my fantasies of solitude and silence fly out the window, but even the time that I'd grown accustomed to spending with God vanished into thin air.

Life for me became a blur of motion, a chaotic jumble of activity from which I had no way to extricate myself. I remember one morning in particular when I stumbled out of bed and into the kitchen to make a cup of coffee, only to discover a massive ant invasion. I wanted to crawl right back under the covers, but my husband, having recognized early on that space was going to be at a premium, had claimed that spot for his morning devotions. Forty-five minutes later, after having dumped the last poison-soaked paper towel in the trash can, I grabbed my stale coffee and headed for the living room to pray.

Collapsing on the couch, I opened my Bible and sat as still as I could while trying to rid myself of the notion that renegade ants were inching their way up my legs. At that moment the baby began to cry, so I closed my eyes and took a few deep breaths, attempting to shut out the noise. By then, however, he'd awakened his three-year-old sister, who came bounding out of their bedroom, jumped in my lap and said, "Grandma, I need some girl love this morning." How could I resist an invitation like that?

And so it was. For eight months, time alone with God was a memory, a remnant of another era when the shape of my life allowed for such luxury. In the beginning, I confess, this brought me no small amount of consternation. Feeling as if my spiritual compass was in perpetual motion, I kept waiting for things to change so I could get back to a *meaningful* walk with God. But as the weeks flew by and things grew more and more unruly, I could only conclude that the Almighty was up to something.

In retrospect I'm certain that God orchestrated those events in my life to break apart some religious preconceptions and rip me away from my comfort zone. He was drawing me into new territory, expanding my borders by exposing my tendency to be far too focused on hours set aside for prayer as the barometer of my relationship with him. What I experienced in ways I'd never imagined was God entering the fray, injecting my busyness with respites of peace in his presence, punctuating my chaos with the stunning sense that he has drawn near.

Several years ago I wrote a book called *The Soul at Rest,* a sort of guidebook for contemplative prayer, filled with tools for those wanting to meet with God far from the madding crowd. Certainly that is one face of what it means to pursue intimacy with Christ. What I hope you'll glean from *Sacred Chaos* is that there is another face, one that lifts our sights to his commitment to come alongside us, to accompany us on our spiritual journey, whatever it may look like on any given day.

The interesting thing is that there is discipline even in this. That is, there are things we can do that will open our hearts to the mystery of God's prevailing presence. To that end, throughout this book, I've provided stories from my own journey and some experiments for you to try as well, such as meeting with God in a one- or a five-minute space. In addition you'll find practical helps, such as suggestions on where you might go to meet with God, given your unique situation, and explanations of how some ancient practices such as fasting or sacred reading can bring freshness to twenty-first-century faith. Appendix A offers thirty-minute and one-hour experiments in prayer, a three-hour mini retreat for regaining balance, and a day-long spiritual pilgrimage for small groups of friends.

The struggle to forge my own path so that I could write this book with authenticity has made me long for others to experience the joy of hearing God beckon through the noise and complications and bluster and stress and monotony of everyday life. I want overworked executives to welcome his whispers in the midst of long company meetings, and sleep-deprived parents to commune with him as they change diapers or rock their babies. I want college students to sense God's presence through the pressure of midterm exams, and people who are energized by motion and activity—who actually take pleasure in life's frenetic pace—to discern his touch in the crowded spaces where they thrive.

My prayer for you as you read—whatever your life looks like right now, no matter what season you are in or how spiritual or unspiritual you feel—is that the things I've written will give you a glimpse of how near God is, causing fresh hope to rise up and confirm that the chaos you call your life can indeed be sacred.

The Quiet Time Fixation

When you come before God, don't turn that into
a theatrical production. . . . All these people making
a regular show out of their prayers, hoping for stardom!
Do you think God sits in a box seat?

MATTHEW 6:5 *(THE MESSAGE)*

No results." Those are the words that popped up on the screen when I decided to do a search for the phrase "quiet time" in my favorite online Bible program. I looked in the Amplified, King James, New International, New American Standard and New Living translations, and there were no results—not one single verse that included that phrase. Not to be dissuaded, I ran a new search, punching in several more versions. Again, "No results." "Quiet time" was simply nowhere to be found.

So I started wondering, how did something that is not once cited in any version of Scripture find its place at the top of our list of things every good Christian ought to be doing? Do you know what I mean? Think about the plethora of seminars and sermons and books and articles on a topic that wasn't mentioned by Abraham or Moses or David or Isaiah or Jesus himself for that matter.

Why has having a quiet time garnered so much attention in Christian circles over the past few decades?

Now, I know what you're thinking, or at least I think I do. If we were sitting across a table talking about this, you would explain to me that while "quiet time" isn't mentioned in Scripture, the spiritual disciplines we practice when we're having a quiet time (such as praying and meditating and worshiping) are. And I would agree. But bear with me as I try to make a point.

The danger with this quiet time fixation is that it can actually end up hindering our intimacy with God. How? Many people, bound by some presumed standard of what a quiet time is supposed to look like, give up before they get started, certain they'll never make the grade. Others get so bogged down with feelings of guilt and self-recrimination about their weakness and inconsistency that they end up avoiding God altogether, certain that he must be disappointed in them. Even those who do manage to master having a quiet time can easily get into the habit of saying amen and then going their way each morning, oblivious to the fact that God wants to speak into the rest of their day, to stay closely connected with them in all they do.

I'm not intent on killing any sacred cows here, but let me pose some questions I've collected from people over the years:

- How many days a week do I need to have a quiet time?
- How long should my quiet time be?
- Do I have to have my quiet time in the morning?
- What are the elements of a successful quiet time?
- What percentage of the time should I spend interceding? Supplicating? Worshiping? Petitioning?
- If I miss my quiet time, can I do it later?

- How can I keep from falling asleep in my quiet time?
- Is God angry when I miss my quiet time?
- How can I get myself to have a quiet time?
- How can I get my husband to have a quiet time?
- How can I get my teenager to have a quiet time?
- How can I get my congregation to have a quiet time?

When I write these all together like this, it seems a miracle that anyone ever manages to enjoy developing a relationship with God. What we need to get our minds around is that as great as quiet times can be, they are only a means to an end. That "end" is an ongoing relationship with Christ that saturates everything—our waking and sleeping, our laughing and weeping, our playing and studying and working and exercising and driving and, yes, our praying.

I wonder what we might think if we could see it from Jesus' perspective. There he stands at the door of our hearts, knocking, waiting, wanting us to know him as our Brother or Lover or Friend, and we get caught up in discussions about how much time is actually enough. He calls our name, intent on pursuing intimacy with us, and we breathe a sigh of relief if we manage to make it to prayer two days in a row. He died that we might know him personally—the very heart, he told us, of eternal life—and we search instead for a workable plan that will enable us to check one more thing off our Christian to-do list. There is something very wrong with this picture.

I talked with a young woman who was so bound up in this area that she couldn't even conceive of time with God being a joyful experience. For years she'd vacillated between extreme discipline and careless indifference, never really connecting with the wonder of what God had for her in their times together. When we met, she was ready to throw in the towel and give up on prayer completely; it was just too frustrating. I probably shocked her when instead of offering the latest and greatest helpful hints, I suggested that she try going an entire month with no "quiet time" at all. What I was trying to do was remove the shoulds and oughts and dos and don'ts that had her tied in knots for years, so that she might finally discover a desire hidden deep within her soul to know the Lord who loves her with an everlasting love.

I'm not suggesting that we throw discipline out the window and resist having any sort of plan for prayer. Clearly, time set aside to meet with the Lord offers blessings we wouldn't want to miss. It can be like drinking a glass of ice-cold lemonade after tilling your garden in the hot sun. Or like finding a wadded-up twenty dollar bill in the pocket of a jacket you haven't worn since last year. Who wouldn't want to experience such things? The problem is that there are days when trying to spend time with God feels more like ripping weeds out of that same garden or balancing a checkbook when there's no money in the account. There is simply no one-size-fits-all when it comes to connecting with the sovereign and often unpredictable Almighty.

> *We are on a journey through the inward space of the heart, a journey not measured by the hours of our watch or the days of the calendar, for it is a journey out of time into eternity.*
>
> Kallistos Ware, in *Disciplines for the Inner Life*

That's why we need to stop treating this particular discipline as a measuring stick for Christian maturity, a work we must get a grip on or suffer the consequence of living in condemnation. More than we realize, there is a self-absorption in this that dishonors God and rebuffs the extensions of his grace we so desperately need. If we can get past all the religious criteria and pressure to perform, we might discover freedom to enjoy him in ways we never expected.

This reminds me of something I read about once called *the two-minute miracle,* which is a technique physical therapists use to help patients overcome their resistance to exercise. They tell them that when they don't want to take a walk, they should say that though they don't feel like walking, they *will* for just two minutes. Then when they finish that, they might tell themselves the same thing again. The point is that before they know it, they're walking and enjoying it and at some point along the way find themselves eager to do the entire therapy plan.

What if we did the same thing with prayer? What if instead of wallowing in guilt or pushing ahead with gritted teeth to get the job done, we tell ourselves we're going to interact with God for just two minutes? Then if we want, we can add another two, and another two, and pretty soon we might discover that we've stumbled into the miracle of a meaningful time in Christ's presence that makes us hungry for more of the same.

I can't help but think that these kinds of authentic experiences, even if hit-and-miss, might bring about a more intimate connection with the Lord than all the well-ordered quiet times of all the duty-driven disciples in this world. Beyond that, God would surely take far greater joy in his children setting aside this fixation with doing it right and instead run to him because he is wonderful and ever worthy—not of a time slot for prayer but of a heart that longs to know him.

MAKING THE CHAOS SACRED

If you're at a place in your life where it's difficult to get alone with God for any reason—time, space or simply a lack of focus, practice the two-minute miracle for the next seven days. Simply look for two minutes a day when you can commune with the Lord. (If at any time you feel like adding another minute or so, feel free!) On the other hand, if you're fairly consistent in spending time daily with God, try going without it for a few days, asking God for some fresh ways to connect with him as you go. You might be surprised at the results.

Redefining Prayer

With all prayer and petition, pray at all times in the Spirit.

EPHESIANS 6:18

Few Protestant pastors are satisfied with how long they pray—at least that's what the results of a survey of 860 pastors recently revealed. Commissioned by LifeWay Christian Resources, the study unveiled all sorts of interesting tidbits, such as the fact that Lutherans and Presbyterians pray more often than members of other denominations and the fact that Pentecostal and Methodist pastors offer longer prayers in general. The part of the survey that got the most press was the news that pastors, on average, engage in prayer for only thirty-nine minutes a day. Reading that made me think about my husband and all the other pastors I know, and frankly something about the whole thing just didn't add up.

I wondered, for example, if the survey's definition of prayer included the hours in which pastors sit slumped at their desk after having studied themselves into a stupor while waiting for God to download the heart of Sunday's message. Or did it count the times they spend processing with God while in the car on the

way to meetings or hospital visits or the dozens of other commitments they have on any given day? Did it take into account the
phone calls that come in regularly, in which ministers find themselves silently pleading for wisdom as parishioners share crises
of mammoth proportions? Did they even ask, I wondered, how
often a pastor awakes in the dead of night and lies there trying to
gain perspective for hours while speaking secretly to the Lord
about the pressures of ministry?

I'm not trying to be defensive here, and I don't question the
notion that pastors—and the rest of us as well—could be on our
knees a lot more, but it seems illogical to reduce a discipline so
highly personalized as prayer to a number in a survey. This, of
course, is what Brother Lawrence—that seventeenth-century
French monk—taught us so well: prayer can never be contained
in forms or rituals, for it is the practice of God's presence in all
of life.

Only in light of this definition will biblical mandates such as
"Pray without ceasing" and "Pray at all times in the Spirit" and
"Give thanks in all things" begin to make sense. Prayer is not
some practice we will one day perfect or a method we can eventually master, but instead it is a lifelong journey of our hearts
awakening to the reality that God is with us. Given the kinds of
chaotic lifestyles to which many of us are accustomed, what we
may need more than anything else are some simple ways to foster greater sensitivity to his continual presence.

Throughout the centuries believers have done various things
in order to be more intentional about this. Frank Laubach, a missionary to the Philippines in the early 1900s, was captivated by
the question of whether a thought of God could take place in his
mind every minute. He deduced that because the human brain

always contained more than one idea at a time, one of them could always be directed toward the Lord. Referring to this as "listening to the inner voice," Laubach came up with the goal of asking God these two questions at least once every minute of the day:

- Lord, what do you want me to say?
- Lord, what do you want me to do?

I have to confess that the idea of doing this minute by minute seemed over the top the first time I read about it, but apparently the practice was picked up by thousands of people after Laubach wrote a pamphlet called *Game with Minutes* in which he told how he moved from failure to a modicum of success in continuously connecting with God. For him, the key was making a conscious decision and sticking with it, regardless of how long it took or how often he failed. The transformation he and others experienced through the little game as a result was profound.

Given my propensity toward legalism, I wouldn't dare try to take on Laubach's plan, although I've found asking those two questions to be a powerful way to connect with God's heart, especially when I'm in conversation with someone or have some free time

> *Can I bring God back in my mind-flow every few seconds so that God shall always be in my mind as an after image, shall always be one of the elements in every concept and precept?*
> *I choose to make the rest of my life an experiment in answering this question.*
>
> **Frank Laubach, *Christ Liveth in Me, and Game with Minutes***

on my hands. A friend of mine makes a conscious effort to check in with God at the beginning of every hour by setting the meeting reminder on his PalmPilot. Some people practice the daily office, a spiritual discipline that incorporates reading through a liturgy from a prayer book at fixed hours from three to seven times a day. The point is that having a prayerful heart doesn't come naturally, and putting some kind of structure or plan in place to help us along can be of great benefit.

Through the years I've done various things to remind myself that God is with me and that he wants to be involved in everything I do. I've put a reminder of spiritual truths in key places such as my bathroom mirror or my steering wheel or even the ceiling above my bed so it would be the first thing I see in the morning and the last thing at night. I've written God's attributes on cards that I carried with me and read throughout the day. I've kept the car radio off for months, making a conscious effort to connect with God during drive time. I've committed to communing with him—worshiping or interceding or sharing my own needs—during household chores rather than letting my mind wander randomly.

To be honest, what these things and others have produced hasn't looked at all like I expected it to. For one thing, there's been a lot less talking *to* God and a lot more listening *for* his voice. Increasingly I have realized that while being with Christ involves sharing my thoughts, more often it means waiting and watching and in essence being *aware*. His Spirit fills all things, and by stopping my noisy chatter, I have grown pleasantly accustomed to the mystery of what it means to serve a present God.

This has also meant growing comfortable with silence, knowing that Christ is with me, even if he is quiet on any given day. In the same way that my husband and I can enjoy being in each other's company without saying a word, so intimacy with the Lord breeds a familiarity free of those awkward moments one feels compelled to fill with conversation. Once I accepted that being attentive to the presence of the Lord was in itself a form of prayer, I realized that my heart connected with his far more often than I had once thought.

Often when I teach a seminar or retreat on prayer, people want to know how long I pray each day (they usually ask how long my quiet time is). I have always felt uncomfortable with the question. The answer I want to give is that I have no idea, not because I haven't been praying but because I have. I want communion with Christ to be such an integral part of my daily existence that I could never assign a measurement to it. I want prayer to be life and life to be prayer, day in and day out. This kind of connecting pleases our heavenly Father and is what our hearts yearn for most.

MAKING THE CHAOS SACRED

Seek to acknowledge God's presence more often during the day in some manner. One possibility is to ask the two questions Laubach asked: "What do you want me to say, Father?" "What do you want me to do this minute, Father?" Remember that the goal is growth, not perfection, so be encouraged with whatever fresh awareness of himself that God gives you.

Kairos Connections

I have set the LORD continually before me. . . .
Therefore my heart is glad.

PSALM 16:8-9

When our son and his family moved out after eight months with us, the life my husband and I were living began to take on some semblance of normalcy—that is, if there is such a thing. In looking back I'd like to tell you that I gleaned all kinds of great wisdom while having them with us, that due to diligence and discipline and an amazing ability to focus on things of the Spirit, my days, like a well-oiled machine, soon ran so well that anyone could see God working right from the center of all that disarray. That's what I'd like to say.

The truth is that through those months of chaos I never did figure out which end was up. Besides having a house full of people, all manner of events made their assault on my time—computer crashes, a jury summons, family medical emergencies and a trip to India with ten high school students. Each of these in its own way wreaked havoc with my sense of well-being and made the notion of personal space seem laughable.

I remember sitting as if in a stupor on those rare mornings when I did manage to make it out of bed before the rest of my family, gulping in the precious commodity of silence like a marathon runner trying to rehydrate before taking off again. Using that time for spiritual disciplines such as prayer and worship and study and meditation—at least in the ways I'd once practiced them—felt impossible.

The ancient Greeks had two words for time. *Chronos* referred to measurable units such as the minutes and hours or days and months that make up our calendars and clocks—the kind of time that, frankly, I lost my grip on during that season. I'm so thankful that Jesus often used the other Greek word for time, which was *kairos*. Referring to quality rather than quantity, *kairos* implies a window of opportunity to be seized and in the New Testament often describes some unique season in the unveiling of God's purposes.

Jesus launched his ministry, for example, by telling the crowds that the *kairos* was fulfilled and the kingdom of God was at hand (Mark 1:15). As he told his disciples to make Passover preparations, he instructed them to find a certain man and tell him that his *kairos* was near (Matthew 26:18). For the Greeks, *kairos* referred to experiences that took place within *chronos* but were not defined by it.

Something wonderful did happen to me during those eight months—God removed my fixation on *chronos* time and replaced it with a fresh awareness of his presence throughout my day. Going without that time with him in the morning each day left me feeling needy and exposed, like being thrust into a storm without proper attire. The result was that I found myself crying out more often for God to make himself real within the chaos.

Before long I began to notice things—nuances I might have missed before—in the words people spoke or biblical truths hidden within ordinary events.

One day, for example, I set out to do some much-needed tending of my garden and decided to get some how-to tips from the Internet. As I read different sites about pruning various kinds of plants, I was amazed when spiritual principles started jumping out at me. Suddenly Jesus' words about his being the Vine and my being the branch that must be pruned in order to bear fruit made sense in a way it never had before. I meditated on those truths and pondered the need for some cutting away in my own heart as I worked in my yard that afternoon. God was breaking in.

I often had the privilege of rocking my grandson to sleep during that season, and I remember being overwhelmed one night as I sang "Jesus Loves Me" for the tenth or eleventh time because

> *There is no event so commonplace but that God is present within it. . . . Listen to your life. See it for the fathomless mystery it is. In the boredom and pain of it no less than the excitement and gladness: touch, taste, smell your way to the holy and hidden heart of it because in the last analysis all moments are key moments and life itself is grace.*
>
> **Frederick Buechner, in *Disciplines for the Inner Life***

I knew I was being immersed in the rhythm of my heavenly Father's love for me. I began to notice the faces of people I passed at the post office or the grocery store or the library, and seeing their pain or loneliness caused me to offer a smile or a word of encouragement, praying for them as I went on my way. One week, as I drove to appointments several mornings in a row, the predictability of the sun spreading its golden blanket over the foothills in our community brought some much-needed peace. God was breaking in.

I remember a day when my first interaction with the Lord happened while I was driving to the gym—it was an apology for having ignored him as I rushed around that morning. I laid out my schedule and asked God to keep me in the center of his will. As I was getting dressed after my workout, a conversation with a friend about my recent mission trip led an elderly Indian woman who'd overhead us to introduce herself. We exchanged phone numbers, promising to keep in touch, and I left with a strong sense that God had broken in, that *kairos* had indeed taken place.

As I am learning more and more to embrace those *kairos* moments, I find a freshness about my intimacy with God. There are days when it seems he beckons so often that I am astounded by it. In truth these occasions are scattered across all the parts of your life and mine—tiny openings where heaven touches earth and the ordinary is graced with a hint of the sacred. I wonder, though, how many we miss along the way, simply for lack of awareness.

The more I've thought about it, the more I'm certain that the God of the universe is never limited by *chronos*. He is infinite— he had no beginning and will have no end—so surely his purposes can't be confined to minutes or hours or weeks or months. He dwells outside *chronos* and yet is ever ready to break into our lives with *kairos*. His interruptions can be as obvious as someone's wanting our phone number or as subtle as a whisper of love, but this I know: holy moments are ours for the taking when we learn to recognize the windows of opportunity God has placed in our path.

MAKING THE CHAOS SACRED

Be intentional about looking for *kairos* moments today. Ask
God to heighten your awareness of the times when he is opening
a window of opportunity in your day—from the people you meet
to the schedule you keep. Use the evening meal to talk about
these as a family, or jot them down before bed each night and
share them with a friend or a small group when you meet.

A One-Minute Experiment in Prayer

There is a beautiful simplicity about learning to seize moments here and there to connect with the presence of the Lord. Even pausing to say the word Jesus on occasion, mulling over what he means to you for a few seconds, can have a great impact. This may not come completely naturally for you, though, so here are a few suggestions that can help you pursue the practice until it is woven into the fabric of your daily life.

- *Be intentional. Start by establishing how many one-minute meetings you'd like to have with the Lord during the day, and then consider ways you might make sure this happens. If this is a new practice for you, start with a small number—three or five at the most.*

- *Be God-centered. One of the most important things we can do is get to know who God really is. It might be helpful to choose a divine attribute on which to focus for a day or even a week (see appendix B). You could then write out Scripture(s) that speak of it on cards and carry them with you. When it is time for your one-minute meeting, these can be a great aid in helping you look to the Lover of your soul instead of your own situation, feelings or circumstances.*

- *Establish "triggers." That is, think of the ways that your normal life can be a reminder to meet with God in the moment. For example, you might tape the card on the steering wheel and plan to meet with the Lord at every red light. You might tape it on your bathroom mirror and meet with the Lord each time you brush your teeth or comb your hair or wash your hands. You could hang it on your bulletin board at work or in your locker at school, reminding you to seek his face regularly throughout the day. If you have small children, you might tape it on their bedroom door, or their highchair or car seat, reminding you to pause and connect with the Lord even as you're caring for them. The key is to have specific ways that will remind you that God is waiting to meet with you.*

• *As you meet with the Lord, take a deep breath, welcome his presence with a few seconds of silent acknowledgement, thank him or praise him for some aspect of who he is and ponder what it means to your life. Present any issue or situation you need his wisdom on. Ask him if he has something to reveal to you. Thank him for his presence. You can do all of this in a minute's time, and before long it will become a habit you won't want to do without.*

As Simple as Turning

It happened that while Jesus was praying in a certain place, after He had finished, one of His disciples said to Him, "Lord, teach us to pray just as John also taught his disciples."

LUKE 11:1

Every now and then a book comes along that challenges my thinking and is convincing enough to make a difference in how I live. This happened to me last year with Anne Rice's *Christ the Lord: Out of Egypt,* the first in a fictional trilogy about Jesus' time on earth. After experiencing a Christian conversion and returning to her Catholic roots about ten years ago, Rice set out to study the Gospels and conduct extensive research into the history, geography and religious underpinnings of the first century. Her passion to know Christ more by pondering his humanity spurred Rice on as she tried to put into words what life for Jesus must have been like as a young boy.

The profound mystery of how Christ operated as both fully God and fully human is something theologians have long wrestled with. Though one of Rice's stated goals is to debunk liberal scholars who deny Christ's deity, *Christ the Lord* is a novel, not a doctrinal treatise. Examining the question of what Jesus understood, and when, and how he related to the world in light of it, Rice's story line posits in a profound way how the tiny child might have experienced a gradual unfolding, a slow awakening in his heart and mind to his destiny, his call and his relationship to his heavenly Father.

As I read I found myself intrigued, asking questions about Christ's humanity that I never had before. Could he have foreseen as a nursing babe, for example, that one day he would hang in a bloody heap on a cross? As a three year old, would he have understood what it meant to possess all authority in heaven and on earth? When he wrestled with his brothers or teased his sisters, could he have grasped that he would one day die to pay the price for their sins? The more I pondered these things, the more I was astonished at the weakness with which the Almighty willingly entered this world.

Scripture tells us that though he was always fully God, Jesus emptied himself to take on human flesh (Philippians 2:5-7). This means he experienced the same raw vulnerability, the same exposure to struggle and pain and heartache and confusion that you and I face every day. While we may never understand completely what this entailed, clearly he did not go through life with his divine nature tucked away like a trump card to draw when things got tough. The Son of Man chose instead to humble himself and live as a human being, full of the Holy Spirit and in absolute dependency upon his heavenly Father.

This is perhaps the most powerful legacy Jesus left us in regard to a life of prayer. So often we're prone to attach grand notions to this spiritual discipline. We're inundated with how-tos on intercession and petition and supplication and meditation and contemplation, and though we want to be praying people, it can feel as if the standard for success has been set way too high. With every new book or sermon on the subject, we find ourselves chafing more and more under the pressure to get it down.

Jesus cut through all that and demonstrated day in and day out that prayer in its simplest form is the natural response to our need, the way in which we express our complete reliance—for strength and guidance and intimate spiritual connection—upon the One who made us for himself. Because he chose to do nothing on his own initiative, Jesus' only recourse was to pray without ceasing. His ear had to be keenly tuned to his Father's voice in order to know what to do and when to do it, where to go, what truths to teach and how to heal or comfort or restore or deliver the broken people who pressed in on him continually.

This Jesus did in the context of a world every bit as chaotic as the one you and I face. With a heart set on accomplishing his Father's will, he cried out for the physical strength, mental acuity, emotional balance and spiritual focus to do so. This meant listening to the Spirit while surrounded by people who wanted something from him. It meant communing with his Father while equipping those who would carry on his ministry after he was gone. It meant maintaining a spirit of prayer even as he dined or slept or relaxed on a summer afternoon with friends. Simply put, Jesus prayed because he needed to pray, leaving you and me an example to follow in his steps.

This is an incredibly freeing reality. Understanding prayer as the natural expression of our need not only honors God as the all-sufficient and sovereign Lord, but it spurs us to come to him as we are, any time and in any place. Letting go of all the trappings, we can live and move and work and play and study and socialize with a posture that holds out empty hands and an open heart to the One who is always willing to pour out grace for the situations we face. Once we really believe that apart from our heavenly Father we too can do nothing, prayer becomes the pipeline through which we receive all that we need to live a life pleasing to him.

Books on spiritual formation often set up ground rules for prayer based on Jesus' life. Some conclude that because he slipped out before dawn on occasion, then morning must be the ideal time to pray. Others point to the nights he spent seeking counsel with his Father, promoting silence and solitude as having the highest value. Still others hold out Jesus' forty-day fast in the wilderness as a standard every believer ought to aspire to. While each of these has its place, they only tell a part of the story.

Far more important than when or where or how long Jesus prayed is the unique and compelling way that he approached prayer. When his disciples asked him to teach them to pray, their only knowledge of the subject had been gleaned from puffed-up Pharisees exacting strict adherence to rules and rituals. Jesus blew fresh wind upon that stale stench of

> *We must learn of Jesus, how He is meek and lowly of heart. He teaches us where true humility takes its rise and finds its strength—in the knowledge that it is God who worketh all in all, that our place is to yield to Him in perfect resignation and dependence, in full consent to be and to do nothing of ourselves.*
>
> **Andrew Murray, *Humility***

religiosity, revealing something far more powerful than a discipline to practice or activity to pursue. Thriving on intimate communion with his Father, prayer had woven its way into the fabric of every part of Christ's life.

This was what the disciples yearned for and the thing that he offers you and me even now—a chance to throw off the weight of religion with all its pressure to perform, to cast aside form and ritual, to abandon every external standard, and learn instead from him, the One who is gentle and humble in heart. He would have us know that there is nothing to achieve, just a yoke that is easy and a burden that is light and rest for our souls as we come before his throne to receive grace and mercy in every time of need.

MAKING THE CHAOS SACRED

Over the course of the next several days, try to tap into the reality that prayer springs from an awareness of your need. When you feel fear or loneliness or stress or confusion or anger or dismay, see these as springboards for prayer, offering up simple pleas for God's intervention. When you are making decisions throughout the day, whether small or large, share the details with God, listening for his voice to guide you.

His Eye upon Us

I will instruct you and teach you in the way which
you should go; I will counsel you with My eye upon you.

PSALM 32:8

Growing up in a large family, I learned early on that I would have to compete for my parents' attention and that even when I got it, it would rarely be undivided. I remember often having the distinct feeling that my mom wasn't really hearing me, even though she nodded knowingly as she went about her household chores while I chattered on. I must have done the same thing to my own kids, because one of my sons used to grab my face and turn it toward his to make sure I was actually listening. Eye contact seemed to be the only real guarantee for him.

Those experiences remind me of the promise from the Psalms where God says he will counsel us with his eye upon us. While I love the idea that the God of the universe is willing to give me his undivided attention, the truth is that there was a time when I availed myself of his counsel primarily on the big stuff, such as what job to take or house to live in or school to attend. I assumed that because my life was committed to him,

God was surely overseeing everything else as well. In recent years, however, I've begun to understand more clearly that the One whose eye is upon me, who watches me every minute of every day, has far more guidance to give if only I'll take the time to listen.

Living with this awareness has had a huge impact on my spiritual journey, but it isn't always easy. It means not only submitting my daily schedule to him but also paying attention as I go, trying to be open to any direction he might want to give along the way. I had no idea until I began to practice this how self-directed my existence had been. I was surprised at how often God nudged me to change my plans or whispered a word in the midst of a conversation or gave me input about things I was trying to accomplish once I opened my heart to his counsel. It has been humbling to grasp the intensity of the connection that the Almighty desires to maintain with me.

> *The Holy Spirit's leadings come with a sense of peace and quiet, even if they point in a really difficult direction which only the grace of the Father can enable one to follow.*
>
> Charles Trumbull, in *His Victorious Indwelling*

Years ago I met a veteran of the faith who habitually took the time to check in with the Lord, regardless of who was around or what was going on. The first time she came to our house for a meal, she spent thirty minutes in an in-depth conversation with our college-aged son while the food grew cold and the rest of us waited for them to finish. She explained later that she felt a strong sense that God wanted her to share some things with him, though she'd never met my son before. As we got to know this godly woman, we realized this was simply the way she lived her life.

She was such an anomaly to me that I remember finally asking her in exasperation, "Do you pray about *everything?* I mean, do you ask God what you are supposed to wear every morning?"

She smiled and said, "Only if I need to."

At the time her answer baffled me, but I think I understand better now what she meant. Her point was that seeking God's counsel is not some kind of legalistic endeavor in which we make sure to check with him about every jot and tittle of our lives, but it is a relationship of such intimate, ongoing communion that we are sensitive to any situation in which he might desire to guide us, even on something as trivial as what clothes we put on. He is the Lord of every part of our lives and thus has the right to speak into any situation and at any point he chooses.

Our part is to tune our ears so that we are sensitive to the nuances of God's voice. This a spiritual discipline that takes time and practice to develop, but the more we open up to the wonder that God's eye is upon us, the more we'll begin to recognize his gentle impressions telling us to stop and listen to what he has to say. As we do so, our intimacy with his Spirit deepens and we become more comfortable with hearing him, enabling us to more readily act in faith on the things we feel he has spoken.

Recently I had the opportunity to share heart to heart with a friend who had been angry with God for many years. The conversation was going so well that I found myself wanting to tell her some things I felt she needed to do in order to open her heart back up to him. Literally as I opened my mouth, I heard these words in my spirit: "Don't go there; it isn't time." I let it go, glad that I hadn't slammed an open door with my friend through spiritual insensitivity. Beyond that I felt a renewed hope for her restoration as I pondered God's personal concern over something as simple as the words I might say to her.

Nothing can bring a greater sense of anticipation to our daily relationship with Christ than the possibility of his speaking into the situations we face or relationships we participate in. From football games to business endeavors, from ministry opportunities to parenting predicaments, from friendships to fun to family vacations and beyond, everything we do has the potential to pulse with the beat of our heavenly Father's heart. As we watch and wait and listen

> *God is not impassive toward us like an unresponsive pagan idol; he calls us to grow into a life of personal interchange with him that does justice to the idea of our being his children.*
>
> **Dallas Willard,** *Hearing God*

for his counsel, we will find ourselves living on the edge of eternity, carried along in the company of the One whose eye is ever upon us.

MAKING THE CHAOS SACRED

Take one day in the coming week and plan to focus on hearing God's voice in it. Spend a little time the night before or that morning laying your schedule out before the Lord. With pen in hand, ask him a few questions, such as these: "Lord, do you want to make any changes? Is there anything I need to be aware of concerning this schedule?" Then offer each situation to him, asking, "Lord, do you have anything to say about this?" If there are any decisions you need to make soon, ask the Lord to speak to you concerning them as well. Then as you go throughout your day, seek to be more keenly aware of those gentle nudges of the Spirit, and when they come, make an effort to listen to what God might have to say.

6

Spiritual Sight

Turning to the disciples, [Jesus] said privately,
"Blessed are the eyes which see the things you see."

LUKE 10:23

I am what they call a left-brained person—that is, if you buy the theory that the two halves of the brain process information in different ways and that each of us has a dominant side. We left-brained people, they say, are more analytical and ordered in our thinking. We make lists and put things into categories and don't usually get the big picture until we've put all the parts together. On the other hand, right-brained folks are more perceptual and intuitive. They tend to think in pictures instead of words and are able to size up a situation with rapid speed. Apparently right-brained people are more creative because they don't get stuck trying to dissect and organize their thoughts—they just go with the flow.

One year I got a book for my birthday called *Drawing on the Right Side of the Brain*. It promised to open up my creative nature by teaching me to disengage the systematic side of my brain. I had to do exercises such as draw with my eyes closed, copy an upside-down image and focus on one square of a picture's grid so I would have no idea what I was actually sketching and couldn't rely on logic. The idea was to recognize how I felt in those moments and then through practice learn to switch from left brain to right. Within days I began to see things differently and was amazed at the colors and dimensions and spaces and shapes I'd never really noticed before. It felt as if I'd been given a new set of eyes.

If we would rise into that region of light and power plainly beckoning us through the Scriptures of truth, we must break the evil habit of ignoring the spiritual. We must shift our interest from the seen to the unseen. For the great unseen Reality is God. . . . But we must avoid the common fault of pushing the "other world" into the future. It is not future, but present. It parallels our familiar physical world, and the doors between the two worlds are open.

A. W. Tozer, *The Pursuit of God*

I thought about this one day when I was reading about Jesus telling his disciples how blessed they were to have eyes to see. They had just experienced the time of their lives as they'd traveled from village to village preaching and healing and casting out demons. Like kids coming out of an amusement park, they couldn't contain their glee as they told him what they'd seen. Jesus must have been excited for them as well, because Scripture says that, overflowing with joy, he thanked his Father for revealing things to them that were hidden from wiser and more intelligent people.

Spiritual sight is an awesome thing when you really think

about it. The eyes of our souls have been opened and a whole new world the Bible calls the *unseen realm* is ours for the taking, one for which we had no capacity before the Spirit of God breathed life into our spirit. It brings us out of our chaos and into the presence of God. The problem is, we forget we've been given such a gift. Like me with my left-brained propensities, we can easily slip into old patterns of interpreting the information that comes our way. Constricted by our humanness, we look right past the goings-on in the spirit realm and don't even know what we're missing.

Jesus set the standard for living with spiritual sight, especially when it came to the way he treated others. Time after time he looked at people and saw things that their friends or family or community couldn't see and then interacted with them accordingly. Out of a large crowd he chose a well-known con man named Zacchaeus to have dinner with, even as the religious leaders looked askance. He defended a woman who broke societal norms to anoint his feet with oil and befriended a prostitute, telling her to go and sin no more. He commissioned a man he'd just delivered from hundreds of demons to be a regional evangelist. And he hailed Simon Barjona as Peter—the rock—though the disciple seemed to be constantly tripping over his own toes.

What if we were to do the same? What if we refused to pigeonhole the people in our lives based on their habits or behavior patterns and began to pray for a heavenly vision instead? What if we stopped expecting others to be what they've always been and asked God what he knows they can be? Think about those you encounter every day—from friends to family to total strangers. How would things change if you started praying consistently for God to open your eyes so that you can see them how he sees them and so that you can see how he might want to work in and through them for his purposes?

A friend of mine decided to pray like this for her employees in preparation for their annual performance reviews one year. She asked God to show her how he had uniquely created each of them, and she was amazed at the things he revealed. As she jotted these insights down, her perspective on the people she worked with every day began to change and she decided to share what she'd received with any who might be interested. Can you imagine coming to an annual meeting with your boss to hear what you've done right or wrong on the job and whether you will get a raise as a result, and being blessed first with a view of how the Creator of the universe might see you? One man was so blown away with what he heard that he threw his stellar performance review on the floor, telling her it meant nothing in comparison.

Praying for spiritual sight in regard to the people in your life can radically change your outlook and impact the way you treat them. Say, for example, that you're worried about your teenager, who has been hauling home an odd assortment of friends lately. What if in prayer you felt impressed that God has created your teen with special compassion for the broken people of this world? Wouldn't this give you a fresh vision for your child's life? And isn't it likely that this would alter the way you look at those friends and how you approach them as well?

Or suppose you get frustrated with your spouse because he or she spends an inordinate amount of time studying and reading up on all manner of subjects. What if God were to show you that he'd instilled a love for truth in your spouse and that he desires to use this for the proclamation of his Word? Would you view your spouse's hobby differently? How might you be encouraged, and in what ways could you spur him or her on as a result of having looked into the unseen realm?

Spiritual sight can make each day an adventure, whether we're sitting in a business meeting or eating out or helping out at our child's school. From the bank teller to the grocery clerk to the college student who files papers in our office, we will see them in an entirely different light if we'll take the time to ask the Holy Spirit to speak some word to our hearts concerning them. If and when he does, we have the privilege of colaboring with Christ in bringing about others' destiny through prayer.

Jesus said we are blessed to have eyes to see—a capacity he grants by grace for his glory. Amazing things happen when we practice using spiritual sight. Average people start looking like saints. Common events become windows into eternity. And our ordinary life teems with holy surprises in his presence.

MAKING THE CHAOS SACRED

Try praying for others by asking God to give you spiritual sight regarding them. Instead of listing things you want for them or think they need, ask God how he sees them and what he desires for them. Take time to listen and jot down on a card the things you hear. Then make this your prayer plan for these people as you seek to see them through God's eyes.

Experiments with Places of Prayer

Something we'll probably need to do often as the seasons of our lives change is to rethink where we might go or things we might do to pursue more focused time with God. Because there is no one-size-fits-all, I've listed below a sampling of ideas that I and others on a similar quest have found helpful.

- *If you drive to work, leave early and spend time with God sitting in the parking lot before going in. Start with fifteen minutes and let it grow from there. One friend of mine did this and by the end of the year was leaving an hour early to pray, lifting up her coworkers as she watched them come to work. (This can be done weather permitting, of course. You might also be able to snag an empty lunchroom or workstation or, if you work alone, your own office.)*

- *If you are a mom or dad with young children, try connecting with God by reading a Bible story or passage and praying with your children before their nap or bedtime (keep it short). Take a few minutes after they fall asleep to meditate on what you have read, asking God to personalize it and speak into your own life.*

- *Find a nook in the local library where foot traffic is minimal. Play worshipful music on your iPod as you pray and read Scripture.*

- *If you are a nursing mom, use the time when you're feeding the baby to read the Psalms aloud or to sing praise songs and worship. This will open up a wide array of personal quiet times!*

- *Go for a walk on your lunch break and talk with the Lord. Print*

Scriptures on cards and carry them with you for meditation.

- *Establish a specific spot in your home and prepare it ahead of time for prayer. Make sure everything you need is there in a box or a basket—a Bible, journal, pen, devotional book, and so on—so you don't have to spend time gathering these things.*

- *If you spend a lot of time in your car, determine to make every drive a unique time to meet with God. Turn your radio off or play instrumental music as you pray and listen to his voice.*

- *Every now and then, as often as your lifestyle and location might allow, go someplace where there are no phones, computers, Internet access or people. Walk in the woods, sit on the beach, wade in a stream or hike into the mountains, giving yourself plenty of time to slow down and connect with the Lord. This will usually require making specific plans well in advance.*

- *If you have a back yard, turn a corner of it into a place of prayer. Install a small fountain, put Scriptures on plaques and include a comfortable lawn chair or bench. In the evening before getting ready for bed, go there and reflect on your day before the Lord. This can even be done during inclement weather—just dress accordingly.*

- *Take a walk in your neighborhood to commune with the Lord. If there is a park nearby, stop and sit for a few minutes with no other goal than to listen to God's voice about your day.*

The key in all of these is to let go of expectations and establish ways that are tailor-made for your situation. When we take the time to make a plan, we're often pleasantly surprised with how easy it is to leave the chaos and enjoy sacred space in Christ's presence.

God in the Bedlam

As for me, the nearness of God is my good;
I have made the Lord GOD my refuge,
That I may tell of all Your works.

PSALM 73:28

He's trying to kill me!" shrieked our seven year old from behind the tree where he'd run from his irritated father while everyone within earshot turned to stare. My husband shook his head, amazed that his decision to discipline our son for a minor infraction had turned into a sideshow for the entire church camp. Counselors and children alike looked on, wondering what their pastor had done to elicit such terror from his youngest child. I won't bore you with the details of that blast from my past, except to say that there was no bodily damage done (although I suspect my husband was sorely tempted a time or two).

Recently I was minding my own business when out of the blue that church camp ordeal came to mind, and I started thinking about how silly it was for my son to have gone around screaming like that. I got to wondering what the people watching really thought, and then I pondered how being a parent can be embarrassing and how being a pastor who is a parent can be even more embarrassing. And that's when then the Lord moved in and disrupted my reverie. In his not so subtle way God reminded me of some ways I tend to resist his attempts to discipline me and how I often bristle at his right to shape my life.

God used a temper tantrum that took place years ago to show me some areas of needed change, which illustrates a principle that makes all the difference in how I approach even the most frustrating and chaotic moments of my life. Simply put, God is in it all. He is sovereign and that means that nothing comes to us without first passing through his hands. But even more important, he intends to use everything—and I mean *everything*—for his purposes.

> *Were we more alive to the fact that there is not an event which happens to us, from morning to night, in which the voice of our Father may not be heard, his hand seen, with what a blessed atmosphere would it surround us! Man and circumstances would then be received as so many agents and instruments in our Father's hand; so many ingredients in his cup for us. Thus would our minds be solemnized, our spirits calmed, our hearts subdued.*
>
> C. A. Coates, in *His Victorious Indwelling*

This is critical because in the course of any given day we can find ourselves dealing with all manner of trying events—from minor disruptions that irritate to issues that could have a colossal impact on our life. And we can get bogged down in these to the point that they become the prism through which we view our entire world. Seeing ourselves as the central character in a story line that has gone bad, we scramble to re-write the pages, not stopping to see where God is and what he might be up to.

In truth, we are part of a story, but it is one that was written before the foundation of the world, one in which the Almighty is both the author and the main character. In pursuit of his own glory, God created the universe to display that glory and for human beings to enjoy it. No longer bound by the chains of self-absorption, as believers we now have the capacity to see him, to experience his presence in and around us, to stand on a higher plane and discover what our role in this grand scheme is and how the things we experience are a part of that eternal drama.

For me, there is no more comforting theological tenet than God's sovereignty. Because (as the psalmist wrote) he is in the heavens doing what he pleases, we can relax about the layoffs at work or the housing market slump or the teacher our daughter didn't want, and we can trust instead that there are good things to be gleaned from each circumstance. We can also get excited about what lies ahead, knowing that if we're serious about living for his purposes, there will be adventures waiting in places where we least expect them.

> *The persons we meet on the pages of Scripture are remarkable for the intensity with which they live Godwards, the thoroughness in which all the details of their lives are included in God's word to them, in God's action in them. It is these persons, who are conscious of participating in what God is saying and doing, who are most human, most alive.*
>
> **Eugene Peterson,** *Run with the Horses*

When our path takes a right turn instead of the left we'd planned, rather than seeing it as a setback or detour, we might find ourselves rejoicing in some divine connection we would have missed otherwise. When our spouse is late and the baby is crying and the dog hasn't been fed and all we want to do is scream, we can take a deep breath, offer it all to God and watch him use that delay to rub off some rough edges of impatience. When we're in a hurry and a neighbor stops us in the street or we run into an old acquaintance at the post office, believing that these encounters are no accident of fate, we can take the time to chat, confident that God will work everything else out.

There are treasures to be had in things like misbehaving children and overpacked schedules and unexpected moves and bosses who rage and bodies that fall apart. God is in the bedlam, and if we want to find him there, we need only learn to stop and listen long enough for him to make his way known.

MAKING THE CHAOS SACRED

As a spiritual exercise, plan once or twice a week to journal each evening about incidents or occasions that did not turn out as you expected. Spend a few minutes in prayer as you do this, writing out the things you believe God might have been doing or teaching you through that experience.

8

Seize the Silence

My soul, wait in silence for God only,
For my hope is from Him.

PSALM 62:5

Only once have I experienced what felt like pure silence. It happened one night as I lay restless in a log cabin, snug under down and sheltered from the cold of an Alaskan winter. The sun had set after showing its face for only a few hours, leaving us with the absence not only of light but of sound as well, for all creatures—human and otherwise—had tucked themselves away as a matter of survival. Something woke me, or perhaps I'd never actually slept, but the silence that had descended was stark.

Try as I might, I could not hear a sound—no crunching feet on hardened snow, no yipping pups around the yard, no wind whispering through the trees, not even the roar of the river, now frozen into stillness. I lay there wide-eyed in the dark, straining to hear something, anything. Finally I tuned in to the rumble of our oil-burning stove in the next room, and soon after that, the rhythm of my husband breathing in and out as he frittered away the night in sleep. How can I tell you what these things meant in the darkness, lying there for God knows how long? Sheer relief came as the two sounds, blending into one, wrapped around me and filled the once-empty space. Like a lullaby, the cadence of it slowly rocked me back to sleep.

Scriptures talk about waiting upon God in silence, and I wonder if what the Lord has in mind is something akin to what I experienced that night. In other words, what if the Almighty has spiritual treasures to impart that can only be heard in the hush of complete stillness? What if when he calls from his holy temple for all the earth to be silent before him (Habakkuk 2:20), he is trying to tell us that there is a gain in the quiet, something valuable we will grasp only when our ears have tuned out the clatter of this noisy world?

This is no simple matter, given the culture in which we live. Silence is not a commodity easily found—or often sought for that matter. We have grown so accustomed to the cacophony of our lives that most of us hardly notice the roar in our ears anymore. We are like addicts who cannot imagine life without the hum of TVs, radios, cell phones, iPods, computers and CD, DVD or MP3 players, to name a few. Noise junkies in search of a fix, we go after this gadget and that, trying to soothe some craving we've never really taken the time to put our finger on. (If you doubt what I'm saying, just turn everything off for a day and see if you don't experience serious withdrawal pains.)

The spillover effect of this in our spiritual lives cannot be underestimated. Acclimated to the steady drone of activity, we can go hours or days or weeks without really quieting our hearts to hear the still, small voice of the Lord. Even when we spend time alone with him, we may find it easier to cram our minds with study and prayers and plans for ministry than to wait upon God in silence. We're restless souls, ill at ease with what feelings or fears might surface, what questions might confuse or what the Almighty might have to say to us if he were to break through the ever-present din.

If only we knew.

I remember a time when for months it seemed as if God had hidden his face from me. Certain I was at fault, I tried pursuing stringent disciplines, took on more ministry activities and sought to release everything I could think of into God's hands. None of it seemed to make any difference. Finally, feeling as if I'd been abandoned, I simply gave up. There was nothing left for me to do but wait. I waited and I waited, and I waited some more, straining through the silence, much like in the darkness of that Alaskan night, to hear something, anything.

I'm still not sure how it happened, or why, but one night, unable to sleep, I was wandering around our back yard and God's voice broke through. What I heard stunned me, for ever so faintly my Lord was telling me, "I love you." How can I explain this? It was the music of heaven, a glorious symphony. Though the message of God's love was one I'd explained, taught, memorized verses about and proclaimed in worship for years, I was ill prepared for the wonder of hearing the Almighty himself singing it over me. It was a holy moment, one whose imprint on my heart remains to this day, though it was gone before I could even catch my breath.

Of all the things God has to say to his children, this may be the message we miss most by not pressing into silence—the sound of him assuring us of his love. Mother Teresa once said she couldn't live even one day without hearing God say "I love you"—that her soul needed that like the body needs air to breathe. I understand this a little more now. Those words have become a lifeline for me, and I know that when I fail to take the time to listen, I'll miss something I badly need to hear.

Seizing moments of silence doesn't come naturally; it is something we have to consciously pursue. These moments are, however, more accessible than we might think. Silence can be found in those final minutes before we drift off to sleep at night or in the early morning as we hit the snooze button and contemplate facing our day. It waits for us in the shower or the car

> *There is no increasing of the pure seed of the spiritual life that does not call for both initial and frequent returns to an island of silence.*
>
> Douglas Steere, *On Beginning from Within*

if we'll we turn off the radio or CD player or put away our Black-Berry. It can enfold us as we sit in a doctor's office or at our desks waiting for some program to load or when we're put on hold during a phone call. It is often there for the taking if we'll just eliminate watching TV or reading the paper or magazines or books for a day or a week or a month.

Whether we find a place of external silence or learn to cultivate quiet hearts in the midst of chaos, one thing that can help us along is what some call *spiritual breathing*. In this practice we take a few minutes to slow our breathing as we mentally inhale the reality of God's presence and exhale the noisy clamor inside us. We inhale the peace of Christ and exhale the anxiety of the day. We inhale cleansing for sin and exhale guilt and condemnation. We do this as long as we need to in order to sense a serenity in our spirits. It is amazing how quickly that can happen through this simple exercise.

Finding that moment of rest is ideal for consciously connecting with the Lord. Once I'm in that place of quiet, I often ask, "Lord, what would you have me know right now? What would you have me consider?" Surprisingly enough, I often hear a specific word for that which lies in front of me. Whether God chooses to direct us each time we wait before him or not, we can be powerfully affected by these respites from the hurried stress of our day.

There are many good reasons for silence—peace of mind, clarity of purpose and focus in the chaos, to name a few. But for those of us who know Christ, there is a gain far more valuable. It is the possibility that we may hear him speak "I love you," wrapping his message around our hearts amid the hustle of life as we know it.

MAKING THE CHAOS SACRED

During the next week, look for opportunities for silence. First, identify various possibilities, noting what changes you might need to make (turning off the car radio, for example). Then work on cultivating these spaces, using them to connect with the Lord. Practice spiritual breathing, thank God for his presence, ask him to speak and then wait in the silence to see what he might say.

9

In Love with the Living Word

I rejoice in your word
like one who finds a great treasure.

PSALM 119:162 (NLT)

Years ago, in an antique bookstore in England, I found a treasure—a volume of letters written by a seventeenth-century Scottish Reformer named Samuel Rutherford. Once pastor of a thriving church, Rutherford had been exiled to a village far from home where he had little to do but spend time with the Lord and write letters to his congregation. These letters were somehow preserved and put into print. One thing I couldn't help but notice as I read through the book was how precious Scripture was to Rutherford. He wrote to one friend about feeling so moved when he read his Bible that he would often lift its well-worn pages to his lips and kiss them.

I've often wondered what makes people get to the point where they cherish Scripture as Rutherford did. While his ardor may have been fanned by the flames of persecution, surely he was most powerfully impacted by the uninterrupted hours he was able to immerse himself in the Bible—a luxury most of us don't have. Given all the things (family and friends and work and community and church) that vie for our attention every day, how can we find a way to integrate God's Word into our lives? What would it take to instill in you and me a passion like Rutherford's for Scripture?

What we may need more than anything is a simpler way of thinking about this critical aspect of our spiritual journey. We live in a time of access not only to dozens of Bible versions but also to scores of study helps. At our fingertips there are all manner of dictionaries, study guides, concordances, Greek and Hebrew lexicons and encyclopedias. The problem is that this plethora of tools, as wonderful as they may be, has promoted a mindset that can make us feel as if Scripture is so complex that any valid approach to it must involve in-depth study. The thought of just picking it up to read seems somehow insufficient, and in fact we may find ourselves avoiding the Bible that lies by our bed or on our coffee table, fearing that we can't do it justice in the time at hand.

An ancient practice encourages us to do just that. It is called lectio divina, or "sacred reading." Based on the belief that God wants to reveal himself to you and me, that he will speak to each of us from his Word in personal, tangible ways as we learn how to listen, this spiritual discipline leads us through four simple steps. Whether we have five minutes or an hour to spend, whether we read one verse or forty, whether riding in the car and reflecting on our kid's Sunday school passage or sitting in a park with a Bible in hand, lectio divina can make our time with God in his Word a deeply meaningful experience.

The first and most obvious thing we do is *read,* not to analyze or study or outline the passage but to slowly absorb the words, pausing as the Holy Spirit nudges us. Being ever aware that God is present to bring his written Word to life, we choose not to allow ourselves to feel rushed or to give in to the pressure to achieve something. We simply seek to be fully present to what we are reading, finding ourselves at times captivated by a single word or phrase, which then becomes our focus as we move on.

The second step is to *meditate,* to take what we've read and ponder it, turning it over and over in our minds as we consider its various facets. Questions we might ask as we meditate include these: *What does this really say? What does it mean? What are the implications of this spiritual reality for my life?* Like narrowing in to a bull's-eye on a target, we eliminate everything but the essential message, which we then reflect on.

Because what we need most is a touch from God, *prayer* is the third step

> *You must become as the bee who penetrates into the depths of the flower. . . . To receive any deep, inward profit from the Scripture, you must . . . plunge into the very depths of the words you read until revelation, like a sweet aroma, breaks out upon you.*
>
> **Madame Guyon,** *Experiencing the Depths of Jesus Christ*

and the centerpiece of lectio divina. William Law, a British Reformer and contemporary of Rutherford, wrote of how we must expect something supernatural to happen every time we approach Scripture. In the same manner that the Holy Spirit originally inspired those words, he must speak to us as we read them. Law insisted that without divine intervention the Bible ends up being no different from any other book we might read.

As we pray, we ask God to open the eyes of our heart so that we might experience the truth of what he has shown us in a personal way. We might offer specific questions about what we've seen or wait upon him in silence, allowing the message to wash over us in gentle waves. We might hold difficult situations we are facing or struggles we are in under the light of this word. We might lift up the people we love or the world at our hands, in our mind's eye seeing the truth of Scripture being applied like a healing balm.

> *The Scriptures themselves can go no further than to direct men to a relationship with God which only the Holy Spirit can give. . . . Therefore the Scriptures should only be read in an attitude of prayer, trusting to the inward working of the Holy Spirit to make their truths a living reality within us.*
>
> William Law, *The Power of the Spirit*

The final step in lectio divina is *contemplation,* which means to focus on being aware of God's presence, drawing near and loving him. If we speak at all during this time, it is to offer words of gratitude for what we've seen or to express the love we feel in our hearts toward the Lord. Often we will sit quietly, even if only for a moment or two, musing over the wonder that the God of the universe has broken into our day with a personal revelation.

While spending protracted time engaging in lectio divina can be wonderful, for many of us this isn't always possible. The great thing is that we can do it in snippets throughout the day, especially since Scripture is readily available on our computers, cell phones and PalmPilots. We can also keep passages on cards or carry a small Bible in our briefcase or purse or stow one in the glove compartment of our car. By becoming familiar with the parts of this discipline—reading, meditating, praying and contemplating—we'll be able to engage in sacred reading whenever we have a few minutes on our hands.

The New American Standard Bible that I use has served me well for more than thirty years. Though a bit cumbersome with its Thees and Thous, it is akin to an old friend to me. While some people prefer to get new ones when their Bible wears out, I'm going to keep having this one rebound—to give it up would be a painful loss. Sometimes I picture my children and grandchildren holding it after I'm gone, trying to decipher the odd assortment of notes I've written in the margins. And yet the truth is that this book will one day join the ranks of every other book—ashes to ashes and dust to dust—for in the end it is nothing more than paper and ink and worn brown leather.

On the other hand, Jesus Christ, the One whose glory shines forth from every chapter and verse, becomes dearer with each passing moment—a reality Samuel Rutherford wrote of often in his letters from exile. It was clear that Scripture was a sacred gift to him primarily because it served to lead him into the warm embrace of the Lover of his soul. Reading Rutherford's letters makes me long for so much more. I want to go further than the places that reading or analyzing or studying or memorizing or teaching God's Word alone might take me. I want to be driven to Scripture by the kind of delight that poured out of that exiled Scottish preacher and drove him to put his lips to its pages.

MAKING THE CHAOS SACRED

Select a passage from Scripture and write it or print it in large letters on cards. On the first card, write out the four parts of lectio divina—read, meditate, pray, contemplate. For the next several days seek to set aside moments for this practice. Remember that you may read only one verse at a time, but your goal is to connect with the heart of God, to hear his voice and to respond in love. You might also seek to memorize a passage as it becomes more and more familiar. You will be amazed at the various facets God reveals as you come back to it again and again.

Experiments in Hiding God's Word

One discipline I've practiced that enables me to connect with God through his Word no matter what my schedule is like is to memorize Scripture, something far easier to do than one might think. Here are some tips I've found helpful:

- *Select a passage that includes several verses or even an entire chapter and print it out in large letters on several cards that you can carry with you wherever you go. (This is easier than trying to memorize a series of different verses.) If you haven't done much memorizing, start with five or six verses, but don't be afraid to add more once you see how manageable the process is.*

- *Work on memorizing whenever you have a free moment. This can be done while waiting in lines, sitting in the doctor's office, riding the bus, working out and so forth. I carry my cards in the car and often use the time spent at red lights to review what I am learning (don't try this while driving!).*

- *Resist any pressure to perform by not putting a timetable on when you'll finish memorizing the verses. Don't worry about how much you master or how long it takes; just be consistent in coming back to it. (I once had a goal of learning the first chapter of Ephesians and ended up memorizing the entire book over the course of a year, something I had never dreamed was possible for me. While I haven't retained it all, years later I'm still familiar with the concepts and where they can be found in the book of Ephesians.)*

- *Memorize one verse at a time, but as you learn a new verse, practice adding it on by reciting the entire passage or chapter up to that point. This helps you retain the context—a great aid in memorizing.*

- *Once you have even a few verses under your belt, engage in lectio divina (see previous chapter) in spare moments here and there, enjoying God's presence as you connect over his Word.*

- *Review all you have memorized from beginning to end in your mind as often as possible. This is a great way to go to sleep each night or to pass the time when you wake up in the middle of the night.*

- *Find a friend who will join you in the process and take turns quoting to each other what you've learned.*

- *Practice saying the passage aloud with dramatic emphasis. If you're really brave, quote it in front of your small group or class.*

10

His Abiding Place

Behold, I stand at the door and knock;
if anyone hears My voice and opens the door,
I will come in to him and will dine with him,
and he with Me.

REVELATION 3:20

Several years ago I read an article in the Home section of our newspaper about people who were designating an area of their house for the pursuit of spirituality. Titled "Sacred Spaces," the piece told of icons, incense burners, candles, prayer beads, religious art and other paraphernalia that men and women were collecting to create a holy atmosphere out of corners or entire rooms. Builders and developers were getting on board, adding appendages to new homes as they tapped into the buyers' longing for a place where, as the article put it, "their soul could feel at home."

When I read that, I found myself reminiscing about the "sanctuaries" I've had in my homes over the years—a well-worn sofa and quiet time basket in the corner of my living room, a table and chair in my makeshift office, and the prayer garden in our back yard where Scriptures on wooden plaques are scattered. Each of these holds a wealth of memories for me, and I'm grateful for the ways they represent the progress in my own spiritual pilgrimage. But the more I've thought about it, the more I'm convinced that though having a set place for prayer is helpful, this alone cannot ensure that we will experience rest or find the spiritual connection we're yearning for.

Deep within us all there is an amazing inner sanctuary of the soul, a holy place, a Divine Center, a speaking Voice. . . . Life from the Center is a life of unhurried peace and power. It is simple. It is serene. It is amazing. It is radiant.

Thomas Kelly, *A Testament of Devotion*

There is an entirely different kind of sacred space to discover, a dimension we can enter at any time and from any location. Transcending the physical and filling our innermost beings, it is called our *soul*—the very substance of who we are, encompassing our mind, our will and our emotions. When Jesus promised that he and his Father would come and make their home in us, he was referring to the moment when his Spirit would enter in, bringing our spirit to life and enabling us to companion with him in the most intimate of relationships for all of eternity to follow. Above all, it is this life that we must learn to cultivate if we want to make something sacred out of the chaos we face each day.

To those of us immersed in a twenty-first-century Western worldview, the idea of communing with God within our souls can seem mystical, beyond our grasp. We're far more comfortable with saying prayers and studying our Bible and attending church services and ministering to others than with entering into the depths of our own hearts to listen to the still, small voice of the

Lord. This requires a childlike trust, a simple faith that is willing to take Christ at his word by practicing his presence, not just in cathedrals or the confines of our devotional life, but in our very being. It means recognizing that the Spirit of God broods within us over every breath we take and every move we make.

Believers have cherished this secret through the ages. In his classic teaching on the spiritual life, Paul wrote that when Christ is in us, God's Spirit communes with our spirit, assuring us that we are his child and praying in our stead when we don't have the words to say (Romans 8:10-16). Catherine of Siena, a fourteenth-century reformer and contemplative, referred to the soul as an "inner cell" and encouraged us to retire there often to be with Christ through prayer. Bernard of Clairvaux, an eleventh-century monk, wrote of the solitude of the mind and spirit where we can interact with Christ even while standing in a crowd.

As a five-year-old girl I "invited Jesus into my heart" and for months afterward tried to work out the wonder of such a thing by drawing stick figures of myself with a cross over my heart. What, I often wondered as I sketched, would Jesus find to do in there while I went to school or rode my bike or took a nap or ate cookies at the kitchen table? Though the perplexities of relating to this God who lives inside me remain, there is a blessed simplicity in knowing that anytime I choose to turn within, he will be there waiting.

Sometimes I think of the hours and days when I have shunned the Lord's indwelling presence through ignorance or neglect or willful rebellion, and I grieve. But I understand better now that no matter how *unsacred* the space within me seems to be, God's desire to make himself at home there far outweighs the waywardness of my heart. He will win. His mercies, new every morning, remind me that though I can never make myself worthy of his presence, I am freely received and fully accepted in the Beloved.

God himself has come to make our souls a haven for holy communion, a place of personal retreat—for rest or rejuvenation or desperately needed restoration—no matter the circumstances that swirl about us. This is both our hope and our destiny, for as Saint Augustine said so well, "The soul is the life of the body, and God is the life of the soul."

When the habit of inwardly gazing Godward becomes fixed within us, we shall be ushered onto a new level of spiritual life more in keeping with the promises of God and the mood of the New Testament. The Triune God will be our dwelling place even while our feet walk the low road of simple duty here among men. We will have found life's summum bonum indeed.

A. W. Tozer, *The Pursuit of God*

MAKING THE CHAOS SACRED

Spend some time thinking about your soul as a dwelling place, the home of God within you. Draw a picture of a house that might represent how you see it. Or make a list of describing words. What makes you want to go there? What makes you want to stay away? Practice envisioning yourself turning inward to meet Christ a few times each day, acknowledging his presence and resting in the reality that he is there, as near to you as you are to yourself.

A Life Small in His Hands

You are my hiding place; You preserve me from trouble;
You surround me with songs of deliverance.

PSALM 32:7

Although it was the end of November, the leaves had turned late that year, making our journey through the French country-side a feast for the eyes. A glorious array of liquid amber, fire-engine red, mossy green and a dozen other colors surrounded us on either side, the gray sky above offering a stark contrast. The villages we passed every now and then with their tall houses and sloping roofs, canal waterways, narrow streets and the ever-present bell tower beckoning from the cathedral made it seem as if we'd stepped back in time.

My friend Julie and I were on a mission to find the birthplace of Madame Jeanne-Marie de la Mothe Guyon. Born in 1648, this woman produced writings that span some forty volumes and that have been translated into dozens of languages, influencing believers from all walks of life to this day. I became captivated by her life and teachings when an aunt gave me her spiritual autobi-ography to read when I was a young woman. Over the years, as I read more of Madame Guyon's books, not only was I amazed at her wisdom and influence, but I gleaned practices from her that altered the way I live my life—things like turning within regularly to listen to the whisper of the Spirit or mentally hiding within the shelter of God's wings when life situations feel unmanageable. I couldn't wait to see the sites where this beloved saint's story had taken place.

Jeanne Guyon's spiritual pilgrimage began as a teenage girl when, though wealthy and widely admired for her beauty, she hungered for something more. Coming from a deeply religious family, she felt dissatisfied with the rituals and mandates that the church handed down, and after experiencing a series of tragic events, she began crying out to God, yearning to know what it might mean to hear his voice or experience his touch. Devoting herself to the pursuit of holiness, she looked everywhere for someone who could tell her the secret of communion with Christ.

One day a Franciscan monk, after having spent several years in solitude, showed up on her family's doorstep, feeling certain that God was going to use him in the conversion of some significant person. Jeanne's father, knowing of her spiritual quest, invited her to come and meet with the man. After Jeanne shared her struggles and her numerous attempts to connect with God, the monk bowed his head, remaining silent for some time. Finally he said to her: "Your efforts have been unsuccessful, madame, because you have sought without what you can only find within. Accustom to seek God within your heart, and you will not fail to find him."

Guyon writes of how those words pierced her soul, how in that moment she was overwhelmed by a sense of God's presence and knew she was changed. From that point forward, her relationship with Christ grew rapidly, and soon people of all ages and from all stations of life were seeking her out for spiritual counsel. As Madame Guyon's influence spread, the government, pressured by the church, accused her of insubordination and heresy, eventually sending her to the Bastille, one of the worst prisons anywhere. Her final years took place in exile, where she ministered by writing letters to people from all over the world, many of which have been preserved and are now in print.

Unlike anyone else I've ever known or read, Madame Guyon understood what it meant to live hidden in Christ, to actively participate *in* this world while drawing her sustenance from the world *of* the soul where he had come to dwell. Whether facing a malicious mother-in-law or a crowd clamoring for her touch, whether experiencing the death of her children or her own disfigurement from small-pox, whether enjoying the friendship of society women or enduring the censure of religious leaders, she found perspective and peace by cultivating the discipline of mentally withdrawing into the sanctuary of her heart. Seeing herself there as one small in God's hands, she experienced a sense of his pleasure that she felt far surpassed any good this world had to offer.

> *When we tell men to seek thee in their own heart, it is telling them to go to seek thee farther than in the most unknown lands. . . . Do they know what it is ever to enter their own selves? Have they ever tried the road? Can they even imagine that it is in this sanctuary within, in this impenetrable depth of the soul, that thou wishest to be worshipped in spirit and in truth?*
>
> **François Fénelon, *Christian Perfection***

While we can connect with God powerfully by turning upward to feast on his majesty or outward to esteem his sovereign reign, a unique experiencing of him comes from turning inward. Entering into this place where his spirit and ours have become one, we find a spiritual focus that enables us to handle life's struggles more effectively and to mine spiritual treasures we might otherwise have missed. Though it takes some practice, we can grow accustomed to hiding in Christ even as we carry on conversations or listen to lectures at school or make sales presentations or get our kids ready for bed or talk with friends or the strangers we meet in the grocery store. This is an immensely practical discipline.

When I first set out to do this, I found it helpful to actually picture myself as being very small in the hand of God. When I got a phone call with some troubling news, for example, I would see myself there and experience an immediate sense of spiritual repose. When others criticized or ignored or rejected me in some way, I would picture myself tucked away in that shelter and would know that I could not take offense. When the stresses of the day escalated and I felt as if I were about to explode, I'd pull myself in and let God enclose me in that place of rest. At some point it became a natural thing to do as I discovered that while the world swirls around me, I can always curl up there, covered by his kindness and strengthened by his love.

The richness of all I'd gleaned from Madame Guyon's life filled me as we visited her hometown that day, but as it turned out, we found nothing there to extol her contribution to Christian history. The office of tourism identified only her childhood home, now an Italian restaurant (where we had a great lunch), but we found no collection of books or letters nor any plaque or monument on display. The cathedral where she had run in the early morning hours to pray as a teenage girl stood regally in the center of town, but it was now locked up, open only once a week for the faithful. The convent where she'd been sent as a child to be educated now housed a bank and showed no sign of spiritual life at all.

As evening drew near and we prepared to leave, we noticed a chateau on a small hill to the north. Because her family was of noble rank, I felt certain Madame Guyon would have spent time there as well, so we hiked up to see what we might discover. Now a college, the castle's sloping lawns offered a vantage point upon the entire town. We stood there for a while, quietly taking in the sights as stories from her life flooded my mind. Every now and then Julie or I would share a thought, but mostly we waited in silence. And then at some point, like a burst of morning light, the truth that Madame Guyon's joy at being small in God's hands was exactly what he had granted her in life *and* in death washed over us both. A sacred hush fell then, and all we could do was stand in wonder at the beauty of such a thing.

In the end there is nothing to tie the lovely town of Montargis to one of its finest daughters, a woman revered today by saints all over the world. I see in this an irony and a grace. That Madame Guyon remains nameless and faceless in her own country, and yet continues to be a source of strength and wisdom and hope to so many through her writings, is perhaps the most significant statement she could have made about the value of pursuing a life hidden in Christ.

Though she surely never suspected the impact she would continue to have, this was a woman who understood at her core how deeply God loved her. She learned through practice that as long as her will was submitted to his, she could find in him everything she needed to face the onslaught of difficulties in her life. Madame Guyon survived and even soared above the tides of life by seeking to hide herself in Christ and commune intimately with him in that place. This is the legacy that lives on, the practice that can change everything for you and me as we discover the secret of being small in God's hands.

MAKING THE CHAOS SACRED

Read Isaiah 40:12 and picture the size of God's hands—wider than the billions of light-years that make up the expanse of the heavens and large enough to hold all the waters and the dust of the earth. This is the God who lives within you. Envision yourself hiding there, remembering Jesus' promise that no one can take you out of his hand. Throughout the next week, as stresses or chaos or confusing events take place, or as people say or do things that hurt you, practice God's presence within by consciously returning to the inner sanctuary of your heart and submitting your will to him to do with as he desires.

Getting Soaked on the Sabbath

If because of the sabbath, you turn your foot
From doing your own pleasure on My holy day, . . .
Then you will take delight in the LORD,
And I will make you ride on the heights of the earth.

ISAIAH 58:13-14

Every single Sunday, along about mid-afternoon, my body goes into shut-down mode. It doesn't matter where I am or what I am doing at the time, as soon as two o'clock hits, I'm completely sapped of energy and start to wilt like a pansy in the summer sun. This has been true for as long as I can remember, and I think I know why. As good Southern Baptists, my family went to church for most of the day on Sundays, with a few hours off in the afternoon. Each week we'd come home from church, eat a lavish meal and then be shooed off to bed by my mom and dad so they could get in some shuteye as well.

For my family and other Christians I knew growing up, Sunday was our sabbath—we kept it holy by not going out to restaurants or banks or grocery stores (except for emergencies, such as being out of milk). And even though we ran like crazy with church activities, we always got those naps in, making it a legitimate day of rest. I'm not exactly sure that's what God had in mind, but it worked for us. Apparently my body adapted so well that to this day I can hardly get by without that Sunday afternoon siesta.

We don't hear nearly as much about keeping the sabbath these days, perhaps because it held so little meaning for many of us in the past. But I wonder at times if in throwing the baby out with the bathwater we've missed something important in our spiritual journey. Is it possible that the sabbath is a gift, given to help us cultivate something our souls need in order to thrive in this world? If so, what is it supposed to look like? How long should it last, and how do we fit it in within the context of twenty-first-century life?

Perhaps the place to begin is with the very first sabbath, instituted by God at the close of creation. While Scripture doesn't tell us explicitly why God took a day off, we do know that he had been in the habit of pausing at the end of each day's artistic venture to reflect on what he'd made, always declaring that it was good. It makes sense, then, that when creation was complete—when he'd finished making starry hosts and whirling planets and humped-back camels and roaring rivers and majestic mountain ranges and creatures in his own image—God would have wanted an entire day to do nothing but gaze out over the entire expanse, to take the time to delight in the wonder of his own wisdom and creativity and power.

Surprisingly enough, this subject doesn't come up again in Scripture until several hundred years later when the Israelites got hungry while wandering around the wilderness and God provided Moses with a plan to feed them. Every morning they would find enough manna for the day covering the ground and on Friday there would be twice as much so that they could rest on the seventh day. That day was to be set apart to the Lord as a perpetual reminder of their covenant relationship with him. God's instructions for it were that they were to celebrate their freedom from Egyptian tyranny by doing no labor of any kind, remembering how he'd saved them with a mighty hand and an outstretched arm (Deuteronomy 5:15). The idea seems to be that they'd be so in awe of all God had done for them that they would need a day to just sit back and enjoy him and his goodness.

Hundreds of years later, Paul wrote that the observance of the sabbath was a shadow and that Jesus was the substance. What does this mean for us? That just as the Israelites were led out of Egypt by God's mighty hand and outstretched arm, so he has redeemed you and me through his Son's death and resurrection—from our sin and this fallen world and the evil one who holds it in his hand. But even more incredible than what we've been delivered *from* is what we've been restored *to*. Because we are new creatures in Christ, the capacity for knowing and enjoying the Creator of the universe, for walking with him in the kind of intimacy he originally intended for humankind, is

> *With Jesus, God's rescue operation has been put into effect once and for all. A great door has swung open in the cosmos which can never again be shut. It's the door to the prison where we've been kept chained up. We are offered freedom: freedom to experience God's rescue for ourselves, to go through the open door and explore the new world to which we now have access.*
>
> N. T. Wright, *Simply Christian*

fully ours. So great must be our gratitude that we celebrate, not one day a week, but every moment of our lives.

This is not to say, of course, that we don't at times need to get away from it all and focus on the Lord. In fact, a case could be made for just the opposite—since through the covenant of grace we are free to find pleasure in all that Christ is, we have even more cause for sabbath getaways than did those who lived in the shadows. This, and the fact that we dwell in a world where motion seems mandatory, makes pulling away for a while our best hope of learning to delight in God in a way that is ours by spiritual birthright.

In order to experience this we're going to have to plan for it, set aside some time to have nothing on the agenda but basking in the wonder of who God is and all he has done. There is a growing movement of people who are returning to the ancient practice of keeping sabbath one day per week for this purpose. Some go to church on Sunday mornings and then seek to extend a sense of holy reverence throughout the rest of the day by not engaging in the sorts of work activities they normally might. Others choose to keep sabbath on Saturday, especially those in ministry for whom Sunday holds far too much responsibility to effectively pull away. Still others take their day off work during the week and alter their activities so that they can enjoy God's presence in various ways.

While I don't keep a weekly sabbath, my husband and I try to get away for a couple of days every now and then, setting aside part of that time to turn off our computers and cell phones and connect with the Lord. What matters is not when or how often we observe a sabbath but being intentional about letting go of the things that hinder us from directing our attention toward God. Whether we engage in a focused study or take a long walk, whether we practice prayer as a discipline or simply rest in the awareness that God is with us, whether we celebrate alone or with family or friends, the keeping of sabbath means taking the time and making the effort to elevate our relationship with the Almighty above all the other pieces of our lives.

Some might call this soaking in the presence of God. *Soaking*—it's a great word. You soak dirty clothes until all the stains come out. When you soak beans overnight, it changes their shape and consistency and even their flavor. Or consider getting soaked in a rainstorm—not just a little damp from a sprinkle here and there, but completely drenched. That's the kind of encounter I think we all need every so often, in the spiritual realm, for our pleasure and the glory of the One who made us for himself.

If you've ever set out to do this, you know all the obstacles that can stand in the way. First there are practical issues such as clearing our calendar and locating a good place and knowing what to do once we get there. Then once we've taken the plunge and made the decision, we may start feeling anxious about all sorts of things. We may find ourselves dreading the silence, fearing what might come to the surface. We may worry about silly things like whether we'll get bored or if God is going to take us to task for the disarray in our lives.

On top of that, when we finally do get alone and quiet, we may feel frustrated at how hard it is to rest in God's presence. Our mind wanders, our body twitches and pretty soon the whole idea that this is supposed to be a refreshing experience seems ridiculous. We may even doze off, feeling terribly unspiritual about it when we wake up. I could go on, but you probably know exactly what I mean.

The good news is that if we'll press into the struggles, things are bound to get better. Through practice, for example, we'll learn how to deal with distracting thoughts. We'll grasp that, like a teacher in a room full of unruly students, we do indeed have the authority to rein them in and settle them down. We'll realize that taking a nap isn't such a bad idea, that falling asleep in God's arms— *holy drowsiness,* as the saints of old dubbed it—is exactly what we needed to help us cease striving and know that Jesus is Lord of all the parts of our lives. We'll discover that he wasn't up there waiting for us to get still so he could hit us over the head with our failures, but that he has longed to reveal his tender, loving care to us in a personal way.

If we keep at it, somewhere along the line we will find ourselves in an encounter with our Redeemer that we've never known before or have long since forgotten. This is the reward, the wonder that can rejuvenate and remind us of all we've been given. Taking time to soak in the presence of God, we'll secure the kind of restoration our souls sorely need and wonder why we waited so long to come. These are indeed blessed sabbaths, experiences well worth going after again and again over the course of our lives.

MAKING THE CHAOS SACRED

Plan a sabbath celebration for the near future. Put it on your calendar and do whatever you can to protect this date with the Lord. Decide ahead of time where you will go, how long it will last and what things you might want to do. Keep the plan simple; be flexible and gentle with yourself. (See appendix A for some ideas on a three-hour experiment in prayer.) Depending on your lifestyle, consider how often you might be able to schedule this kind of time and begin planning even further in advance for the coming year.

Experiments in Physical Prayer

When people in Scripture prayed, it was often accompanied by a particular physical posture—hands raised, head bowed, lying prostrate, kneeling, dancing, clapping and so on. A spiritual practice that is unusual but can prove surprisingly helpful for those willing to push past the awkwardness and try something new is using physical movement in a more focused way in prayer. Children love learning these kinds of prayers. Likewise, adult small groups benefit from praying together in this intimate way.

I've provided two examples for you to try, but feel free to make up your own. I learned the first one from a friend, and the second is taken from an Internet site that offers many options. Either one can be done whenever you have a few minutes to yourself, but they can also be the starting point for a lengthy time alone with the Lord.

Physical Prayer 1

- *Sit quietly with your hands in your lap. Take a few deep breaths to calm your spirit.*
- *First focus: God in every place. Use your fingertips to draw a wide horizontal circle in the space in front of you. Say quietly, "God, you are here," affirming that he is present in every place at every time. Ponder his omnipresence.*
- *Second focus: God with me. Lift your arms straight up above your head and bring them down, one hand resting on each shoulder. Say quietly, "God, you are here," affirming that he is present in the room with you, as real as any friend who might come to visit. Ponder the comfort in this.*

- *Third focus: God in me. Bring your hands together and place them over your heart. Say quietly, "God, you are here," affirming that he is present within you by his Holy Spirit. Ponder the wonder of this.*

- *Say quietly, "I worship you. You are Lord of all." Worship him in silence.*

- *Do this a few times, pausing at each step for as long as you need in order to experience the wonder of God's vastness and his tender intimacy.*

Physical Prayer 2

- *Stand up with your arms straight out to your side and your palms pointing to the ceiling and pray, "Creator God."*

- *Bring your hands together in front of you, forming a triangle with your thumbs and forefingers, and pray, "The three in one."*

- *Keeping the triangle shape, bend down, placing your hands on the ground, and pray, "Be in this place."*

- *Stand up again and place the triangle over your chest, praying, "Be in my heart," and over your forehead, praying, "Be in my mind."*

- *Take the triangle above your head and pray, "I love you and adore you." Bring your hands down to the starting point and start to pray again.*

- *Repeat this as many times as you wish. Try altering the speed at which you pray this body prayer and developing your own words or actions.*

13

Consolations for the Hungry Heart

When my anxious thoughts multiply within me,
Your consolations delight my soul.

PSALM 94:19

When my husband, Joe, and I were dating in college, we attended a small Bible study every Tuesday night. Joe, quiet by nature, usually sat back and took everything in, rarely jumping into the fray. Then something happened that changed all that. As he tells it, we were studying about the indwelling Christ when suddenly the reality that the Spirit of God actually lived within him hit like a lightning bolt. Overwhelmed and unsure what to do, Joe quietly left the meeting and went outside, where joy exploded in his chest. Soon that once-reserved teenager was running and jumping, tears streaming down his face at the wonder that the God of the universe inhabited his heart. He was never the same again.

That night Joe experienced the *manifest* presence of God, something saints throughout the centuries have called *consolations* (taken from the New Testament word for the Holy Spirit, often translated as "Comforter"). While God is omnipresent and never leaves us, there are times when he chooses to reveal himself to us personally in ways that are hard to put into words. While these can be dramatic, more often they are like a gentle breeze that blows in, leaving us keenly aware that something supernatural has happened. We may glimpse God's majesty in some stunning way or sense the sweetness of his love in our innermost being or find ourselves overwhelmed by the beauty in a well-known Bible verse. Consolations are gifts that God gives by enabling us to experience what we would have missed otherwise.

> *The Presence and the manifestation of the Presence are not the same. There can be the one without the other. . . . If we cooperate with Him in loving obedience, God will manifest Himself to us, and that manifestation will be the difference between a nominal Christian life and a life radiant with the light of His face.*
>
> A. W. Tozer, *The Pursuit of God*

What does this have to do with crowded schedules and busy seasons, with overstuffed days and weeks, with meeting the demands of family and work and church? In other words, how do consolations fit within the chaos we call our lives? Simply this: when push comes to shove, one of the first things that tends to go is our intimate connection with God. Though we may continue to put our time in—going to church, reading the Bible, praying for people or doing some other ministry—we can find ourselves anxious and dissatisfied, living with a sense that all is not as it should be. If we're not careful, we may drift into a spiritual monotony that impacts our outlook on all of life.

Consolations remind us that God intends far more for us than commitments and duties and habits and routines. He means for us to *experience* him, to taste and see that he is good, to take in his glory and know the tenderness of his touch. Every now and then we may need to stop for a spiritual reality check, making sure that our relationship with him hasn't been reduced to something that lacks the wonder of his revelation upon it. If this is the case, what we must do, and indeed all we can do, is to come humbly before God and begin asking him to make his presence real once again.

There is, however, a paradox about the ongoing quest to experience God in tangible ways that can make the process a perplexing one. It is simply that though he calls us to diligently seek him and delights when we do, God does not always give us what we long for. This became clear to me once after I'd had some incredible times with him during a season of prayer and fasting. When the feelings of joy began to wane, I prayed harder, fasted longer and cried out again and again for him to show himself to me as he had before, but the heavens were silent.

One day a college student came to visit and told me about the most extraordinary experience she'd had. Having gone to sleep one night asking God to help her understand what his glory really was, she'd woken up with a start. The next thing she knew, she was on the floor, facedown in worship amid many tears. As she describes it, the weight of God's presence was so strong that she couldn't move for hours. Still feeling the effects, she trembled as she spoke of it.

I listened in awe, rejoicing with her as she shared, and yet at the back of my mind was the nagging thought *Why her? Why not me?* Hadn't I been asking and seeking and knocking again and again in prayer, while she'd barely uttered one request? Over the next few days I saw how subtly I'd believed that it was up to me, that I could somehow earn God's favor by praying long enough or hard enough until he would have no choice but to give me more of himself. The reality I had to come to terms with was that God, in his sovereign wisdom, was not going to bless me with a greater manifestation of his presence at that time, regardless of all the spiritual calisthenics I might employ.

What believers over the centuries have come to understand about consolations is that they are a means to an end, that God uses them to draw us to himself so that we will honor him through hearts that delight in him. Yet because in our human-ness we can so easily slip into seeking experiences instead of the One who bestows them, there will be times when he withholds tangible expressions of his presence. His ultimate desire is to pu-rify our faith, to bring us to a point where our love for him doesn't depend on how we feel or the experiences we might have but on who he *is*.

In a book written in the fourteenth century by an unknown au-thor, called *The Cloud of Unknowing,* this process of purifying our faith is viewed as a holy calling, a blessed pursuit in which we leave behind elementary things and cling to God alone, directing the longings of our heart toward loving him, not for what he can do or has done for us, but for the worthiness of his very being. The cloud of unknowing that stands between us and God can be pierced only through desire for him alone. As we set aside our insistence upon understanding his ways or experiencing his hand upon our lives, God—by his grace—draws us into that cloud where we can offer our love, unfettered by our need.

When I first read that book and other similar books many

years ago, I found them baffling and wondered if they would ever make sense to me. At the same time, I was tantalized by how much there was to learn, how vast the terrain of God's glory really is. Like Isaiah's temple filled with smoke or Ezekiel's fiery chariots or John's vision on the isle of Patmos, these were like landmarks far down the road, reminding me that there would always be more, that my entire life on earth and into eternity would be a journey of discovery.

Today I understand a little more what it means to pierce that cloud of unknowing. I know the blessing of experiencing God's consolations. I've trembled under the weight of his touch and wept at the wonder of his magnificence. I've also learned what it means to wander through the wilderness where God's presence came at last like a refreshing oasis in that dry and weary land. I've lived

> *Although it be good to think upon the kindness of God, and to love Him and praise Him for it; yet it is far better to gaze upon the pure essence of Him and to love Him and praise Him for Himself.*
>
> **Anonymous author of *The Cloud of Unknowing***

through a dark night of the soul when no matter what I did or how I cried out to God, I could not feel his touch or hear his voice for months on end. Yet still the Lord has been faithful, for through all of this my heart has only grown to want to know him more.

Over the course of our lives we all must learn to navigate our own path through the ebb and flow of God's manifest presence. There will be times when the busyness of life has dulled our hearts and closed our souls to the wonder of his revelation, when what we need most is to seek the Lord until he grants us the joy of experiencing him once again. But as we grow in Christ, there will also be seasons when God calls us to live by faith alone, when—no matter how great our desire—he chooses not to show himself to us in tangible ways.

In the end each of us will have to live with the paradox of thirsting for a God who alone determines when and how that thirst will be quenched. We must learn, then, to treasure his touch and yet trust him in the silence, to yearn for his presence and yet honor him through dryness and darkness, to enjoy those moments when Christ seems near and yet esteem his worth when we cannot find him. We do this ever aware that consolations—as wonderful as they can be—are but a foretaste of that blessed day when we will see our Lord face to face and spend eternity getting our fill of his glory.

MAKING THE CHAOS SACRED

As you walk through the day, ask God to open the eyes of your heart to manifestations of his presence. It might be something as simple as experiencing a sweetness about knowing him. It could be something you read that moves you or a word from a friend that has the touch of the holy upon it. Or it might be something powerful enough to bring you to your knees in awe. Journal about what you experience, talk about it with a trusted friend and ask God what he desires of you in response. If you are in a dry or dark place in your journey, take the time to list consolations you've experienced in the past. Spend a few moments in silence reflecting on these, then respond with simple expressions such as "I love you, Lord," or "You are worthy."

14

Into the Depths

O LORD, You have searched me and known me.
You know when I sit down and when I rise up;
You understand my thought from afar. . . .
[You] are intimately acquainted with all my ways. . . .
Search me, O God, and know my heart;
Try me and know my anxious thoughts;
And see if there be any hurtful way in me,
And lead me in the everlasting way.

PSALM 139:1-3, 23-24

Water was pumped into my childhood home from a well in the back yard—something every family in the neighborhood had. One year ours went dry, as wells are wont to do, and we had to dig a new one. I remember the excitement the day the large drilling machine was brought in. For hours the noisy thing bored deeper and deeper while the men stood around making bets about how many feet into the ground it was going to have to go. Load after load of dirt and debris, of rocks and sand and clay, came pouring out until at last the cry went up that they'd struck clear water. Though that was only the beginning of a lengthy process, I remember the look of relief on my dad's face in that moment as we all celebrated our good fortune.

I read once that there is water to be found across the entire earth's subsurface for anyone who will dig deep enough. That started me thinking about our souls and the fact that Jesus said his Spirit would settle in our souls like an underground spring from which we can drink whenever we feel thirsty. So often, however, it seems as if the well has run dry. Prayer feels like an exercise in futility and the words of Scripture are lifeless and bland. Worship becomes perfunctory and it's hard to remember what it was like to have a sense of God's touch on our lives or the satisfaction of his presence quenching our spiritual thirst.

What we may need in times like these is a spiritual excavation to bore down through whatever rocks and sand and slimy debris might be keeping us from drinking from the wellspring of his Spirit in our souls. A monk named Ignatius of Loyola established a practice in the sixteenth century called the *prayer of examen,* which enables us to do just this. Consisting of five parts, the exercise helps us look back over a period of time—a day or a week or a month or more—and hear God's voice concerning the sinful patterns of behavior or harmful heart attitudes that may be standing in the way of our intimacy with Christ.

Believers have practiced the prayer of examen as Ignatius taught it for more than four hundred years, perhaps because of its simplicity and the value in each component. It begins with a time of quieting the heart and thanking God for all he has done. This sets the tone for the exercise by taking our eyes off ourselves and putting them onto him. As we thank God, even for small things, something changes inside us. An antidote to self-absorption, gratitude enables us to regain perspective on the world in which we live and on our own spiritual need.

The second step in the prayer of examen is to ask for divine illumination into the condition of our heart. This is critical because our tendency is to focus on more glaring issues, never realizing that these may be indicators of something deeper that God wants to deal with. I remember, for example, how as a young wife and mother I often lost my temper when things got out of order at home. I would feel horrible about my impatience and anger, but no amount of confessing—to God or my family—seemed to change anything. In exasperation I begged God to show me *why* I kept getting so upset over inconsequential things. The Lord slowly and gently began to dig through some layers that had formed over my heart through years of life experiences.

The first things I saw were anxiety and fear. When the normal stresses of life came, I tried to assuage an inner panic by controlling everything around me, down to the messes my kids made. I needed God to reveal what I was really afraid of, what false assumptions I was operating under and how these led to the more visible sins. Ultimately God brought me to a place of repentance for my lack of trust in him, for my failure to believe he would provide and for my taking responsibility for things that belonged in his hands. This was the beginning of a freedom that has grown steadily through the years, but I know that without the work of the Holy Spirit I would never have gotten to what I really needed to address.

The third step is to look back over a specific period of time and to see where God's presence has made a difference and where we have fallen short, either through neglect or through willful disobedience. Some examples of questions we might prayerfully consider are these: Where have I seen God's hand at work in me or through me or around me? Where have I missed what he wanted me to see or know? Have I spoken unkind words to anyone? Have I displayed a lack of faith through anxiety or stress? Have I treated people as Jesus would, especially those in my own family? Were there any opportunities to show mercy that I missed? The length of time we might look back upon can vary, but the shorter the period, the more specific we'll be able to be and thus the greater our opportunity for change. Daily or weekly examen is a valuable asset to our spiritual journey.

> *Few souls understand what God would accomplish in them if they were to abandon themselves unreservedly to him and if they were to allow His grace to mold them accordingly.*
>
> **Saint Ignatius of Loyola,** *The Spiritual Exercises of Ignatius of Loyola*

The fourth part of this spiritual discipline is to ask and receive God's forgiveness, something well worth making the conscious effort to do. While Jesus has paid the price for all our sins and forgiven us even for those we've not yet committed, you and I need the cleansing and renewal and restoration that can come only by acknowledging our need and the wrongs we've done. Through our confession the Lord releases us from a sense of indebtedness and enables us to experience the flow of his Spirit once again.

The final part in the prayer of examen is perhaps the most important one, for it tests our willingness to change. Having confessed our sins, we repent, which means we choose to walk in the opposite direction in the future. In the case of my frustration and anger at home, for example, I determined that whenever I started to feel those tinges of irritation, I would stop and take a deep breath, removing myself from the situation if need be so that I could let God's Spirit calm my heart and show me what the nature of my fears really were. I also made plans to meditate on Scriptures such as Philippians 4 (which suggests replacing anxiety with prayer) and Psalm 37 (which instructs us, instead of fretting, to trust in the Lord and wait patiently for him). Choosing to take specific action steps is an important and fitting way to end this spiritual exercise.

The prayer of examen can be a valuable part of daily life, enabling us to walk in more constant communion with God. Because there is an eternal spring of living water rippling through you and me, we can rest assured that though we may feel dry and distant from the Lord at times, we never really are, for the source of refreshment is only a prayer away. As we learn to excavate regularly, we'll discover that while it requires patience and practice and can at times seem difficult, this discipline is worth the effort to secure the free flow of God's Spirit into all parts of our lives.

Making the Chaos Sacred

Take some time to practice the prayer of examen. (You may need to start with an extended period if you are in one of those times of dryness or distance from the Lord or if it has been a long time since you've done anything like this.) As a reminder, here are the five steps:

1. Calm your heart and give thanks to God.
2. Ask the Holy Spirit to illumine your heart to what is needed to excavate your heart.

3. Look back over a period of time and look for sinful behavior or harmful attitudes, continuing to ask God for wisdom as to what may be below the surface behavior.

4. Ask God's forgiveness and receive his full cleansing.

5. Prayerfully commit to specific steps you can take to walk in the opposite direction of the sins you have seen.

As you get more familiar with this process, you'll be able to go through it quickly, incorporating it into your life several times throughout the day, as the Spirit leads.

New Practices

I discipline my body and make it my slave, so that,
after I have preached to others, I myself will not be disqualified.

1 CORINTHIANS 9:27

What can we do when the things that once energized and brought us joy in the Lord have become rote or dull? When disciplines that have served us well no longer seem to be producing fruit in our lives? How do we handle the boredom that rises up on occasion in our relationship with Christ? The reality is that, because God is infinite, we'll never attain anything close to fully knowing him. And yet there are times for each of us when it feels as if we've hit a dead end in our relationship—or worse yet, that we're going backward. What are we to do during these times?

Perhaps, instead of seeing seasons like these as setbacks, we ought to approach them as springboards to a different phase in our spiritual journey, as opportunities to open our hearts to fresh ways of growing in grace. Spiritual inertia—a malaise we all face at one time or another—can be a catalyst for developing disciplines we've never tried or may have thought were beyond our capability. By attempting something new, we just might find ourselves moving forward with anticipation of what God has in store, instead of being paralyzed by confusion or frustration or self-condemnation.

This idea of needing some kind of new spiritual habitat reminds me of something I read once about hermit crabs. When unsuspecting parents buy these cute little pets for their children in the kiosk at the mall, they may not realize that before long the crabs will outgrow the shell on their back and have to go in search of one that is more roomy but not so heavy that they can't comfortably carry the thing around. Of course that's nigh onto impossible for a crustacean in suburbia. So pet stores now offer a wide array of intricately painted shells in assorted sizes, which owners can buy and place near the crab for its impending expedition. Similarly, when you and I feel unsettled or constricted in our relationship with Christ, perhaps what we're experiencing is a need to move into a new and different structure—one that can accommodate the growth spurt God intends but that won't crush us with its weight.

I experienced this several years ago. I'd been through a season when my life was chaotic and my heart had grown ambivalent about spiritual things. I kept trying to squeeze in quiet times, but they were of little value as I'd find myself bored by the Scriptures and distracted in prayer with the details of the day at hand. Then one day I read of a way to pray that seems to have originated with the desert fathers, men who left pagan society in the fourth century and went to the desert to live and seek a purer relationship with Christ.

Such a prayer is called a *breath prayer,* and the idea is to choose a phrase that is simple and heartfelt and can be offered to the Lord in one breath. The words might be something from

Scripture, such as "Create in me a clean heart, O God," or "You are my Shepherd; I shall not want," or they might articulate a more personal need. Breath prayers can be for our own benefit or be offered on behalf of others we know. Once we've decided on the particular phrase, this then becomes the focus of our communion with Christ for a season. Some people like to repeat the prayer numerous times as they breathe in and out, quieting their heart before the Lord.

When I read about breath prayers, I decided to give it a try, asking God for something that would accurately reflect that particular season of my life. Almost immediately I heard the words "Give me a heart for you," and I knew this was what I wanted and needed most—a renewal of yearning for the Lover of my soul. Taking a deep breath, I exhaled and said softly, "Give me a heart for you." Then I tried it again. "Give me a heart for you." And again. "Give me a heart for you." By the third time, it felt as if that simple prayer had become a part of me. Like one of those hermit crabs finding just the right shell to inhabit, I was ready to move into my new spiritual discipline.

For the next few weeks, I offered my breath prayer in all kinds of situations. I prayed it at red lights and while waiting for my kids to get to the car after school. I prayed it as I combed my hair and folded clothes and stood in the grocery line. I prayed it as I got dressed and as I worked out at the gym. Each night when I went to bed, those words—"Give me a heart for you"—were on my lips until I fell asleep, and I often awoke in the darkness or at dawn with the clear sense that they were still there.

What surprised me was how quickly things began to change. Within days I found myself thinking about God often, wanting to spend time with him and eager to read his Word. A peace settled in around me and I knew instinctively that he was near. This was incredible to me, having struggled with spiritual dryness for so long. Perhaps even more amazing is the irrevocable manner in which God answered that breath prayer. I don't know exactly when, but at some point my passion for him became strong and I found myself filled with desire to know him more intimately and to live for his purposes. Though I've experienced ups and downs in my spiritual life since then, I can honestly say that my desire for God has never waned as it did before that first breath prayer experiment.

There are a few things that are helpful to remember when we are embracing new spiritual disciplines, whatever they may be. First, we need to examine our hearts before we embark on them, allowing God to reveal unhealthy motives. One of the greatest mistakes we can make is to believe that our efforts will somehow curry favor with him, that the harder the discipline and the more diligent we are, the more pleased God will be with us. Soon we are carrying around a burden God never intended for us to bear. The Pharisees, for example, believed everyone ought to follow their zeal in keeping the sabbath, and so they sought to weigh people down with a multitude of regulations concerning it. When Jesus broke the rules, their pride was hurt and they took offense, to which he responded, "The Sabbath was made for man, and not man for the Sabbath" (Mark 2:27).

If Jesus were here today talking to you and me about spiritual disciplines, I suspect he might say the same thing—that they were made for our benefit. In other words God did not create you and me because he needed people to serve him with our works but so that we could know him and enjoy him and glorify him as a result. Things like prayer and study and meditation and contemplation and fasting were made for us—they are tools to help us grow in intimacy with him. This perspective relieves the pressure we often feel to master a discipline and frees us instead to anticipate all we have to gain.

Another thing to remember is that whatever spiritual discipline we choose needs to be a good fit for us at the time. We are ever prone, as human beings, to want more from ourselves, to think we should be so much further along than we are. Like a hermit crab who adopts a shell too large for its body, we'll walk around weary of the weight and unable to find a way out.

Recently I was talking with a young man who felt he could not possibly get alone with God. When I asked him how much time he thought was necessary to do so, he told me he'd always felt like a failure unless he could spend at least an hour. As we walked through his day, it was clear he was on overload, so I asked him if he thought he might be able to devote just five or ten minutes before bed to reading a psalm, singing a song of worship and offer-

The ordinary purification and healing, whether of the body or of the mind, takes place only little by little, by passing from one degree to another with labor and patience. . . . The soul that rises from sin to devotion may be compared to the dawning of the day, which at its approach does not expel the darkness instantaneously but only little by little.

Francis de Sales, *Introduction to the Devout Life*

ing the next day to the Lord. Though it took some convincing that even this small amount of time would produce growth in his relationship with God, he finally agreed to give it a try.

When I saw him the next week, he was elated at how God had met him in those short sessions before bed each night. Within a couple of months, he discovered that he needed and really wanted more time in prayer, and he began looking at things he could change to get it. The point is that he found a discipline that worked for him in the place he was in, and once he was completely at home with it, he realized that he was ready for something more.

We can learn one more thing from those hermit crabs. Sometimes one of them waits too long to venture out and look for a home. And then, when it can't find a home fast enough, it dies, unable to protect itself from the weather and oceanic warfare. God has destined you and me to a path of continual growth in him. When we feel the danger of stagnation looming, we must move forcefully to expand our horizons, to look for some new structure so we can continue on that path, protecting our hearts from the battle at hand. Spiritual disciplines are something we cannot survive without, and once we really get this, we'll find great joy in pursuing whatever ones God has for us.

MAKING THE CHAOS SACRED

Acquaint yourself with various spiritual disciplines and begin making plans to try something new. For beginners, there are several described in my book *The Soul at Rest*. I also highly recommend Richard Foster's *Prayer: Finding the Heart's True Home* and Tony Jones's *The Sacred Way*.

Five-Minute Experiments in Prayer

*One habit that takes minimal effort but can produce great re-
sults is to develop a discipline of taking time when we awake and
when we lay our head down to sleep to connect and commune
with God. The saints of old called this recollective prayer and
saw it as a way of bringing all our thoughts and plans under the
sovereign hand of our Lord. While you may plan other five-
minute spaces throughout the day, beginning and ending it in
God's presence lays a foundation and establishes a perspective
that will affect your entire day. You may want to keep a journal
by your bed to jot down words God speaks, direction for specific
situations and so forth. Here are some suggestions for establishing the practice:*

Upon Waking

- *Plan to spend your first conscious moments in communion
  with the Lord. If you wake up before your alarm, or if you don't
  normally set one, quietly affirm that God is present with you
  as soon as you begin to stir, thanking him that he has been
  there throughout your night. (If you wake up to an alarm, seek
  to quiet your mind first by taking a few deep breaths.)*

- *Spend a couple of moments acknowledging the beauty of
  Jesus, perhaps by focusing on one of his many names in Scripture. You may want to plan for this in advance by choosing
  one name to focus on for a week or more (see appendix C for a
  list with Scriptures).*

- *Consider your time spent sleeping. Did God speak in any
  way? Did you have a dream that may have spiritual signifi-*

cance? Pray about these things. (A good habit to get into is to write down dreams that might mean something as soon as you awake, or even during the night, and then pray over them in the morning.)

- Offer the Lord your day as you quietly ponder the plans you have. Seek his face for any words of guidance or encouragement. Listen for his voice.

- Thank God for all that he will do this day. Ask him to make his presence known in and through you as you interact with others.

Before Going to Sleep

- Praise God for the ways he has blessed you today. These can be anything from food and drink to answers to specific prayers. Try to name at least five things.

- Look back over your day as you commune with the Lord. Ask him to reveal any ways in which he worked in and through you, and thank him for these. Then ask if there are occasions of sin or disobedience. If there are, receive his forgiveness and cleansing.

- Ask God to speak to you about those on your mind—your children, spouse, roommates—and pray for them accordingly.

- Offer your own sleeping hours to the Lord. Affirm that he is your protector, that he never slumbers nor sleeps. Ask him to speak to you even as you rest—in revelations or dreams. Ask God to enable you to awaken mindful of his presence.

Unholy Moments

Have mercy upon me, O God, according to thy
lovingkindness: according unto the multitude of thy
tender mercies blot out my transgressions.

PSALM 51:1 (KJV)

There are times in the life of every believer when it feels as if we're failing miserably, when our sins have piled up in our hearts like dirty socks on laundry day. Maybe we've been beset by run-of-the-mill transgressions such as snapping at our kids or swearing at another driver or vegging out on dreadful TV shows or fuming at our spouse. Worse yet, we may be guilt-ridden over shameful acts done in secret, such as viewing Internet pornography or cheating on our taxes or drinking too much or spending more money than we have on things we don't need. Whatever the case, the idea of talking to God, of freely coming into his presence in light of our condition, seems almost embarrassing. We'd like to pray, but all we can think of is that we ought to have something better to offer the Lord, something holier than . . . well, holier than we are in this moment.

That notion plays in my head like a bad sermon—or I guess I

should say, a lot of bad sermons—I heard as a kid. In the church of my childhood, though the details changed from week to week, the preaching almost always reminded us about what great sinners we were and how disappointed God must be as a result. The underlying theme seemed to be that until we could do something about this, we weren't candidates for communion with him. This kept me spinning like a hamster on its wheel, and still, after all these years, I am my own worst enemy, pointing the finger at myself and feeling crushed beneath the weight of a burden I cannot bear.

When failure flaunts itself in my face, I forget that Jesus has no use for my religious ranting, that he intends to expose it for the sham it is. The lie that my behavior could ever disqualify—or qualify me for that matter—to come before God is sheer lunacy, given his holiness. This is what Jesus clearly laid out in the story of the two men who went to the temple to pray. The religious leader, feeling good about his week, started thanking God for all the things he had done right and for all the bad things he *wasn't,* including a tax collector like the man nearby. The tax collector, on the other hand, stood alone, eyes cast down as he cried out, "God, be merciful to me, the sinner" (Luke 18:13). This man knew his own heart, but rather than obsessing over his sins in some sort of spiritualized self-pity, he did the only thing possible—he threw himself on the mercy of God.

Believers throughout the centuries have made that penitent's words their own, from its simplest form ("Lord, have mercy") to its most complete ("Lord Jesus Christ, Son of God, have mercy on me, a sinner"), understanding that this is the only realistic grid through which to approach our relationship with God. Whatever the things that make us feel loathe to come to him, however we've violated the life of his Spirit within us, it reminds us that he is still merciful, ever ready to pour out forgiveness and compassion upon needy sinners who will come as they are. This alone enables us to run *to* the Lord instead of *from* him, no matter how great our sense of unworthiness.

While the Orthodox Church began as early as the fourth century to teach people to offer this prayer regularly, calling it the Jesus Prayer or *prayer of the heart,* widespread use of it as a spiritual discipline flourished when a nineteenth-century Russian pilgrim wrote a book about his quest to learn how to pray without ceasing. Over the course of a year, as he traversed the land alone, he was profoundly changed by uttering those words— "Lord, be merciful to me, a sinner"—silently from his heart thousands of times a day. Scores of Christians since have embraced this practice as both an antidote to sin and a preventive measure against it.

People employ the Jesus Prayer in a variety of ways. Some recite it over and over for several minutes each morning; others repeat it as many times as possible during hours set aside for solitude; and still others make it an integral part of their ongoing internal dialogue with Christ. It is not, as some might suggest, akin to offering meaningless repetitions or a ritual that simply makes us feel better. We are asking God for mercy. In Greek the word is *eleēson,* which has its roots in the term for olive oil, something used to heal many diseases in Christ's day. By expressing those words—"God, be merciful to me, a sinner"—we are participating in a spiritual transaction that can heal us from the inside out, having significant long-term effects on our lives.

For me, the Jesus Prayer has become a natural way to set my

heart on the Lord, especially during the more unholy moments in my day. When I feel my schedule spinning out of control or a friend has let me down or I'm stuck in traffic far longer than I'd planned or I've lost my keys or the refrigerator is on the blink or I'm frustrated with my spouse or tired of being a mom (the list goes on and on), instead of trying to be better than I am or more spiritual than I feel, I simply acknowledge the truth that I'm a sinner in need of God's tender compassion that very instant. The blessedness is that he always comes through and my outlook changes.

Let all multiplicity be absent from your prayer. A single word was enough for the publican and the prodigal son to receive God's pardon. . . . Do not try to find exactly the right words for your prayer: how many times does the simple and monotonous stuttering of children draw the attention of their father! Do not launch into long discourses, for if you do, your mind will be dissipated trying to find just the right words. The publican's short sentence moved God to mercy. A single word full of faith saved the thief.

John Climacus, *The Ladder of Divine Ascent*

I've found one of the most helpful times to offer the Jesus Prayer is when I'm at risk of taking offense at something or someone. Living in a culture of entitlement, we are all too protective of our rights and can easily become frustrated or irritated when we feel they've been violated. We often go around letting these things smolder like a slow-burning fuse, until eventually they ignite an explosion in us that spills out on everyone around. Taking offense, no matter how slight the affront, not only keeps us from revealing the humility of Christ to others, but also shuts our hearts off from God so that we can no longer enjoy the peace of his presence for ourselves.

Several things can happen if we choose instead to pause, take a deep breath and slowly pray, "God, have mercy on me, a sinner," once or twice or as many times as it takes to set our soul's gaze upon Christ. It reminds us, first, that our God is always merciful, an ever-present help in time of trouble, a soothing balm to our anxious spirit. Second, admitting our own imperfections and propensity to sin enables us to see the offender in a different light, making it difficult to continue to fret or be angry with them. And third, like the penitent in Jesus' story, we can bask in the knowledge that we've been restored to a right relationship with God, and we can go our way justified in his sight.

While there are still times when I want to run from the Lord because I've failed or am tempted to give in to my sinful desires, I am learning the simple pleasure of coming to him just as I am, no matter how impossible the situation or how unworthy I might feel. The Jesus Prayer enables me to stop trying to get it right first, trying to be good enough or spiritual enough or holy enough, and rest instead on the promise that my Lord is ever willing to pour out mercy on this sin-sick soul.

MAKING THE CHAOS SACRED

Begin practicing the Jesus Prayer by meditating on its meaning throughout the day. Offer it silently under your breath whenever you feel a tinge of distress or are tempted to take offense at someone else. If you wake in the night and cannot sleep, practice doing the following. Breathe in deeply, saying, "Lord Jesus Christ, Son of God," then breathe out slowly, saying, "Have mercy on me, a sinner," until you fall asleep again.

The Heavens Declare

The heavens are telling of the glory of God;
And their expanse is declaring the work of His hands.

PSALM 19:1

As a kid, I loved the creation story. I can still see myself sitting in the circle on the floor in Sunday school while our teacher placed the various cutouts on her flannel board as she walked us through the six-day process. Day one, light. Day two, heaven. Day three, earth and sea, trees and plants. . . . You get the point. The big moment, of course, came on day six. That's when they would put the figure of Adam and Eve up on the board (their naked bodies discreetly hidden behind a hedge) and would tell us about God's favorite thing: men and women.

What I usually came away with was a sense that the reason creation took place was because God got lonely. Apparently (it seemed to me) he grew tired of hanging out by himself for multiplied millennia and wanted someone to talk to, a pal to hang around with, to have some laughs with and in general to keep him company. This made perfect sense to me back then. Being the middle child of five and often feeling like the odd man out, I

knew what it meant to be lonely, and I felt sorry for God, especially after he had to send Adam and Eve packing.

Of course the truth is that the all-sufficient God did not create
the world or its inhabitants out of any sense of need. The God-
head—Father, Son and Spirit—in perfect delight at the glory of
his own being, formed mountains and trees and waters and birds
and beasts to put his power and creativity and wisdom on display
for his own joy. By forming men and women in his image, he im-
bued them with the capacity to know him intimately, not only
through personal re-
lationship, but also
through the magnifi-
cence of all he'd
made.

From night to day, from day to night,
The dawning and the dying light
Lectures of heav'nly wisdom read;
With silent eloquence they raise
Our thoughts to our Creator's praise,
And neither sound nor language need.

Isaac Watts, *Psalms and Hymns of*
Isaac Watts

What this means is
that one of the best
ways for you and me
to get to know what
God is like is by
opening our eyes and
looking at the world around us. The heavens, one psalmist wrote,
are continually declaring his glory, pouring forth speech day after day about who he is. Observing this isn't always easy for those
who live where the sounds of traffic drown out birdsong or smog
obscures the sunset or exposure to animals is limited to a cat
sleeping at the foot of the bed. It's even more difficult if our lifestyle means pulling out of our garages day after day, only to be
swallowed up by them again several hours later.

But still, whether we live in some mountain resort or on a city
street or out in suburbia, Paul tells us that God's invisible at-

tributes—his eternal power and divine nature—can be plainly seen through the things he has made. What we may need, then, is to be more intentional about looking for these within the context of the life we have.

I realized this recently after having returned from a vacation in New Zealand, where the mysteries of creation were on full display everywhere we looked. Because the trip was a gift from our church, I'd promised to take lots of pictures. So, armed with my son's digital camera and a memory card that could hold up to a thousand shots, I found myself snapping constantly.

I remember one day in particular when my husband and I were both taken aback by the intricate detail on the wide variety of trees with their vast array of colors. We paused often and took loads of pictures, our hearts full of thanksgiving for such beauty in that place far away. When I came back home, I found myself noticing several trees on my own street that I'd somehow missed before, and I began to think about what it would be like to visit my town as a stranger, camera in hand. What would I notice? What images would I want to preserve in this place if my senses hadn't been dulled through years of ordinary life?

God is always putting himself on display, and I, for one, can easily miss the show. Can you imagine him watching, waiting for you or me to sit up and take notice of the birds that nest in the eaves of our office building or the wildflowers scattered by the freeways we traverse daily or the stars sprinkled like fairy dust across the sky on a moonless night? Nature in all its grandeur exists for this purpose—to reveal its Maker in such a way that our hearts, full of joy at what we've seen, will explode with praise and thanksgiving for letting us in on such a thing. What we may not realize is that our own happiness is enhanced through the process.

C. S. Lewis calls this the "appointed consummation" of joy. In a book of reflections on the Psalms, he wrote of how he struggled with the idea that God commands us to give him praise, until one day he realized that people naturally want to praise the things they value—from mistresses to mountains, from weather to wine. We do this, Lewis surmised, because our delight in what we've seen isn't complete until we express the way we feel in some way. The point is that you and I were made to respond to oceans and rivers and rocks and hills and horses and geese and geraniums, and the only appropriate way to do so is to worship the One who made them. Not only does this give him the glory he deserves, but also it brings a satisfaction to our souls that we cannot experience any other way.

An insect and a star, the mildew on the wall and the cedar on Lebanon, a common laborer and a man like Augustine, are all the creatures of God; yet how dissimilar they are, and how varied their ways and degrees of glorifying God.

Abraham Kuyper, *Work of the Holy Spirit*

I once read about some scientists who compared the earth to a peach, noting that we've gone no deeper than the bloom on it in penetrating the mysteries of the created order. This reminds me that my capacity for joy through what God has made is like a bottomless well. Think of it. No matter how much we take in of his glory—through creation or any other way—we've only just begun. Regardless of how deep we go in our understanding of his character and his ways, we will only have skimmed the surface of his infinite being.

This energizes something in me. It makes me want to foster an explorer's spirit, to develop the kind of drive that will keep my senses tuned to the mysteries that await me. I know they are there—these whispers of wonder—from the warmth of a summer breeze to the spiny lizards in my back yard, from a shooting star to the sound of a thunderclap on a stormy night, from the agapanthus and impatiens in my garden to the earthworms that wriggle across my sidewalk after a spring rain. I want to open my eyes and see this world, so that I can more fully savor the glory of the One who made it and experience the consummation of joy he has intended for me from the beginning.

Making the Chaos Sacred

Think of your normal day or week. When might there be opportunities to connect with God through nature? Can you take a walk at lunchtime? Sit under the stars after dinner? Set a goal to be more intentional about doing this as you go, asking God to reveal himself in things you might normally take for granted, such as the sunrise or a windstorm or the scent of the flowers that bloom in your yard. Take the time to offer words of praise, remembering that your joy isn't complete until that takes place.

Immersed *in* a World I'm Not *Of*

They are not of the world, even as I am not of the world. . . .
As You sent Me into the world, I also have sent them into the world.

JOHN 17:16, 18

I once saw a T-shirt at a missions conference that bore the slogan "What part of GO do you not understand?" The slogan implied a frustration with believers who were ignoring the mandate to go to the nations with the gospel. Though I love missions and empathize with the slogan's sentiment, it risks reducing the Great Commission to something I'm not sure Jesus intended. The term he used when he told us to go literally means "as you continue on your journey," indicating that wherever he might lead us to live—on a foreign field or in our own hometown—his charge to share the good news should fit well within the context of our everyday life.

In other words, when we sit in corporate meetings or stand in line at the bank or attend our child's piano recital, we are "going." When we mow lawns or make beds or file taxes or work out at the gym, we are "going." When we take vacations or chat with a neighbor or sit through a PTA meeting, we are "going." The challenge is to recognize that Christ's command to preach the gospel converges in the places where we find ourselves and among the people we encounter every day.

This means that, instead of walking around with blinders on, we will open our eyes to the opportunities God is placing in our path. It means that instead of cloistering ourselves with like-minded people, we will seek to coexist comfortably with those who might disdain the things we hold dear. It means we will determine not to shy away from the tension that comes from living in a world we are no longer of. These things are not always easy to do.

I saw this illustrated in a graphic way years ago while on an overseas mission trip to India. With a nine-hour layover in Calcutta (Kolkata), our team had decided to visit the hub of Mother Teresa's ministry. The city, named after a Hindu goddess of death and destruction named Kali, proved to be every bit as fascinating—and far more disturbing—than the folklore surrounding it.

We rode in vintage taxis from the airport—fifty-year-old leftovers from the British occupation—with diesel fuel burning our eyes and throats as its fumes filled our lungs. As we inched along amid the pandemonium of cows and cars and rickshaws and buses competing for space on the narrow roads, it felt as if the city was engulfed in shadows, physically and spiritually. The air was thick with humidity and strange scents. Scores of people lined the streets, despair etched on many of their faces.

After close to an hour, the driver stopped abruptly in the middle of the road and pointed to a nondescript horseshoe of buildings. A nun greeted us at the door and told of various ministries we could visit—a home for the dying, a hospice for AIDS patients and a home for abandoned and crippled children, all within walk-

ing distance. She encouraged us to come back within a couple of
hours and join them for chapel, where perhaps we'd be able to
meet Mother Teresa.

The intensity of the taxi ride across town was nothing in comparison to that six-block walk to the orphanage. Forced to press
our way through the crowds, we tried to ignore the vendors
hawking their wares, the insistent beggars and the occasional
body of someone hovering near death beneath our feet. I walked
as close behind another team member as I could, staring straight
ahead and avoiding eye contact, as if by not looking I could blot
the misery out of my mind.

At the orphanage we showered affection on babies who were
blind, deformed, palsied and diseased, and all too soon it was
time to walk back for evening prayers. Though we did have the
privilege of meeting Mother Teresa before we went in, this did
little to assuage the discomfort I felt in that city so foreign to anything I'd ever experienced. Yet, as we stepped through a door
into the room where the nuns knelt on a concrete floor, it felt as
if we'd entered another world altogether. Clad in white habits,
the sisters raised their voices in beautiful harmony as they sang
praise songs on their knees.

We entered and sat in the only space available—the ledge of
an open window where the car horns honked at our backs,
shouts of vendors filled our ears and the heat and odors of the
city continued their relentless assault. It felt as if we could almost
touch the presence of God in the room before us and yet could
not escape the squalor and oppression from the streets behind.
While the liturgy was moving and made us want to stay, the open
window reminded us that soon we'd have no choice but to go.

In the years since, I've often experienced the same kind of

struggle that I felt that night in Calcutta. Contemplative by nature, I find it easy to hide away within the safe haven of God's love, to shut myself off and ignore the world beckoning at my back. My head in a cloud, I walk through life straight ahead, avoiding contact with the masses of broken people, sheep without a shepherd who press aimlessly beside me.

What strikes me most about the incarnation is that Jesus, knowing what awaited him, left the portals of heaven and came to a place in which the ugliness of sin and the stench of death and hopelessness must have assaulted him constantly. Willingly, he embraced a darkness that must have settled in his pores and burned his eyes, the fumes of our depravity filling his chest with every breath. But still he came into a world in which he surely never felt at home and chose continually to live and love and immerse himself in it in every way.

So we go. We go to our neighbors whose children have measles and our teenagers who cannot seem to keep their rooms clean. We go to our spouses who need an en-

All the world is one great sacramental loaf. We are not—nor will we ever be, God save us— solitary intelligences spinning in the dark void of space. He crowds upon us from Sheol to the sea; he jostles our thoughts along the pathways in our brains. He hides in the bushes, jumping out in flames to startle us into seeing. He sequesters himself in stables and swaddling so as to take us unawares. He veils himself in flesh, the same flesh that drips into my fingers at the end of my arms and sprouts into hair on my head.

Virginia Stem Owens, in *Disciplines for the Inner Life*

couraging word and our friend whose life is spinning out of control and our coworkers whose stories about their weekend leave a bad taste in our mouths. We go to serve a meal to the homeless or lead a Bible study in the local jail or mow the lawn of a single mom recovering from alcoholism. We plunge fully into a world that will never feel like home to us again because Jesus said that as the Father sent him, so he has sent us. We go because we alone have the privilege of carrying salvation's story, the hope every heart needs and many souls yearn for even now.

We go. And because we go, this world that we are no longer of becomes a holy place as we bear Christ's presence in it.

MAKING THE CHAOS SACRED

As you walk through the next few days, look for the places where it seems God's presence is least likely to be found. Then ask him to give you his perspective, to show you what it might mean for you to be sent there, just as he was sent into the world. Keep a journal of these opportunities for a few days as you focus on his presence without.

Experiments in Creative Ways to Fast

Jesus' words on fasting can be narrowed down to a few basic principles. First, it isn't to be some super-spiritual event that draws the attention of everyone around us. Second, fasting offers unique gains for our spiritual life. And third, it is a way to express our desire for more of him (Matthew 6:16-18; 9:14-15).

In my experience fasting is one of the most effective ways to jump-start my spiritual life or to move me to a new level of intimacy with Christ. I may not always experience the full import of this change during the fast, but I have never failed to see some change in the days to come.

On a practical basis, one of the reasons fasting works is because the pangs of doing without something remind us to pray. While Scripture speaks of fasting as abstaining from food in some manner, this is not always possible for us, given our hectic lifestyles. I believe that anything that is so integral to our lives that we will experience the loss when we do without it can serve the purpose of fasting. To that end, here are a few ideas for fasting as we go.

- *Turn off the radio, CD player or iPod for one month. Use the silence as you drive or work around home or at the office to offer simple requests to the Lord, such as "I need you" or "Speak, Lord, for your servant is listening."*

- *Go without visual media—TV, Internet, movies and so on—for a month or more. Use the time to connect with the Lord by reading Scripture meditatively and interceding for the needs of others.*

- *Eliminate some food or drink that is prominent in your life, such as soda, coffee, pastries or chocolate, for at least a month. Let the cravings for them draw you to seek God's face. Use the time you would have prepared or purchased these foods to commune with the Lord. Keep track of how much money you would have spent on them, and give it to the poor.*

- *Engage in a word fast by minimizing your verbal responses. Whenever you would naturally offer your opinion or a question or chat, instead listen to the conversation of others while you are communing silently with the Lord. (Share with others ahead of time why you are doing this so they'll know what is going on.) You might do this one day a week for several weeks.*

- *Put aside reading materials, even Christian books, for a month and use the time instead to read God's Word without any concordance, study notes or other helps.*

- *Give up personal computer use one day per week or one week per month. Use the time to pray and seek the Lord through his Word. (Let others know that you won't be checking e-mails and so on.)*

- *Leave your cell phone at home for one day a week and use the time when you'd normally be talking with others—whether driving or waiting in line somewhere—to talk with God.*

Practicing the Presence of People

The Word became flesh and blood,
and moved into the neighborhood.
We saw the glory with our own eyes,
the one-of-a-kind glory,
like Father, like Son,
Generous inside and out,
true from start to finish.

JOHN 1:14 *(THE MESSAGE)*

A few years back, in response to a challenge from a Christian speaker, I signed up to volunteer at a hospice for men dying of AIDS. The experience was unsettling from the moment I met the caretaker at the door on my first visit. After she introduced me to Noel, a young man who had no friends or family to walk with him through his final days, Noel and I went out on the porch to visit so he could smoke. He began to share, still grief-stricken, about losing his partner, whose ashes were scattered in the bay far below us, while I fidgeted nervously, trying to figure out a way to interject spiritual truth into the conversation. Though I didn't succeed that day, I left with the hope that I'd be able to share at some point and Noel would have the opportunity to turn his life over to Christ before he died.

Things didn't exactly pan out the way I'd hoped. Noel suffered from dementia, which meant we were rarely able to carry on a coherent conversation. The one time I was able to share about my own relationship with the Lord, he did show some interest, and I was eager for our next visit. But when I arrived the next week, I found out that Noel was in the hospital suffering from injuries received in a drunken brawl. How he'd managed to get himself to a bar was a mystery, but when I finally got to see him a few weeks later, Noel could barely move, much less talk. From that point forward he deteriorated daily, both physically and mentally.

On weeks when Noel couldn't get out of bed, I would sit and hold his hand and regale him with stories of my son's escapades at school, which elicited little more than a weak smile every now and then. On one visit when he was able to get to the porch, he spent the entire time trying to light used cigarette butts so he could have a smoke. The next week I brought him a pack of his favorite Marlboro Lights, something that—though I knew the Spirit had led me to do it—went against every bone in my Baptist body.

And then one day the caretaker met me at the door to tell me that Noel had died that week and was already buried in an indigent's grave in a location they couldn't disclose to me since I wasn't family. I left, surprised at my feelings of overwhelming loss. Over the next several weeks I found myself trying to fit the experience into some kind of grid that made sense, brooding over what my purpose had been, especially since Noel seemed mentally incapable of responding to the gospel from the start. Before long it became clear to me that my season in that place was God ordained, that I was there for my sake and *his* more than anyone else's.

Recently I was reading Mike Mason's book *Practicing the Presence of People* and I began to reminisce about the things I learned through my experience with Noel. I thought about Jesus' words that whatever we've done to the least of these, we've done to him, and I wondered how many of us believers grasp the full import of what he meant. Do we realize, for example, that our love for him is commensurate with our ability to have compassion on human beings he has made in his image? Do we really believe that practicing the presence of people who seem to have nothing to give in return enables us to experience the presence of the transcendent God in a tangible way?

These are some of the truths I came to embrace during my time with Noel, even as I recoiled at the motives of my own heart that each visit exposed. I realized early on, for instance, how I spend far too much time practicing my own presence with others, wondering what they think of me or how I can impress them. With Noel, this would have been laughable. Most of the time, when I talked, he gazed off into the distance as if I wasn't there. When he did manage to join the conversation, his comments rarely had anything to do with what was on my mind. Week after week, as I was forced to deal with the depths of my own self-absorption, I began to view Noel differently, to experience compassion for him as a person and wish I'd known him in some other time and place, before the ravages of disease had stolen the life from his soul.

I still remember the crystal blue of his eyes, the way they would be vacant for the longest time and then suddenly light up for no apparent reason. Sitting here right now, I can almost feel the weight of his fragile body as I helped him into my car for a picnic one day. Years have passed and yet I remember the sound of his halting voice as we sat in the park and he insisted that God would never want him, given the mistakes he'd made. I cried on the way home that day, pleading for a miracle that would never come. And yet God's presence in my car as I wept was strong—a bittersweet memory that has no fit within the confines of much Christian dogma.

I saw as well, over those months, how goal-oriented I tend to be, how my commitment to go the distance with others is often fueled by an expectation of how they are going to act or change or grow as a result of my efforts. If people reject my not-so-subtle assumptions about what they need, or if they don't measure up to my standards of success, I can easily turn aside, confident that I've done my part. The worse Noel got, physically and mentally, the more I wanted to wash my hands of the whole situation, often pleading with God to release me from going. He never did. But at some point I began to notice that I was looking forward to my time with Noel, that I was actually becoming eager to get there each week. I understand better now that the experience I'd somehow stumbled into was joy—not in what I might accomplish, but in the act of loving itself.

Though as believers we will always long to see God's power bring hope and light and change to others, when we give of ourselves on the basis of what might be gained, no matter how lofty or spiritual the goal, we run the risk of contaminating love with manipulation—something people can usually smell a mile away. God's ways are so far above ours that it is foolish to think we are the ones to determine what he must do, how he must do it and the timing of his work in someone else's life. The simple truth is that he calls us to love—to love him with all of our hearts and to love others as ourselves. And when we do, we will find our hearts most keenly in tune, not only with their presence, but with Christ's as well.

One of my last memories of my time spent with Noel is of a Christmas party I threw for the entire hospice. Rounding up an assortment of friends and family members, I traipsed into that house with the group on Christmas Eve bearing platters of homemade goodies, toiletry-filled stockings and a wrapped robe and slippers for each of the men. Normally it would have been impossible to drag them all out of bed at once, but that day they came—in walkers and in wheelchairs and on canes, some of them slow of step and others confused in mind, but each one ready for a party that promised a limitless supply of sweets.

Our tendency is to run away from the painful realities or to try to change them as soon as possible. But cure without care ... makes us preoccupied with quick changes, impatient and unwilling to share each other's burden. And so cure can often become offending instead of liberating.

Henri J. M. Nouwen, *Out of Solitude*

We sang and read the Christmas story while the men ate and opened their presents, and for a few minutes that day the dark loneliness that normally characterized the place dissipated. I remember sitting there watching how much fun everyone was having and feeling thankful for Noel and the months we'd spent together. Looking at the men's faces reminded me of how Jesus taught us to throw parties for the folks who couldn't throw one back—for the poor and the crippled, the lame and the blind. That is, for people a lot like these men.

Jesus went on to say that we shouldn't worry about getting anything in return, that we'd be paid in full on resurrection day. But
as I celebrated Christmas with those eleven men dying of AIDS,
I felt as if I were receiving my reward in full. There was something
sacred about hanging out in that hospice with those hurting souls,
about practicing the presence of each one and feeling the heart
of Jesus beating alongside mine. It was love, pure and simple.

MAKING THE CHAOS SACRED

Make a conscious effort in the coming days to demonstrate love
in a tangible way to someone who can give you nothing in return,
even someone who may never respond in spiritual ways. As you
do, consider that Jesus is present in that act, that he has said that
it is as if you are doing it for him. If you have time, keep a journal
of your experiences and of what you learn about him through
those experiences.

The Gospel Without Words

This is a large work I've called you into,
but don't be overwhelmed by it. It's best to start small.
Give a cool cup of water to someone who is thirsty, for instance.
The smallest act of giving or receiving makes you a true apprentice.
You won't lose out on a thing.

MATTHEW 10:41-42 *(THE MESSAGE)*

A few months ago a friend and I came home to find my nine-teen-year-old son and a group of his friends in our garage trying to fashion his shoulder-length hair into a Mohawk with six-inch spikes. Using a razor and all manner of gel, they were not having much luck getting the edges straight or the spikes to stand up. When my son asked if I could help, I was speechless, not yet having gotten over the shock of the whole thing. Ideas flooded my mind—of what people were going to think of him *and* me when they saw him sporting the new do. Then, repenting under my breath for my fear of others' judgment, I shrugged at my friend and took the razor in hand. For the next thirty minutes, we la-bored together to perfect a spiked Mohawk on my son's head.

As we cut and shaped and blew-dry the gel-slicked strands, I remembered how God had brought Jonathan to us as a baby through adoption. And I pondered how it must have felt for him to grow up as a person of color in a fair-skinned family. I considered his passion for all things technological and how the rest of us couldn't begin to converse with him in that strange language he'd mastered. I thought about what it was like for him to be a pastor's son, about the pressure he'd surely felt to live up to a standard that others set and often expected.

Then I reminisced over the past few years in which he had been trying to find his own way, his interest in spiritual things having waned. I knew that more than anything God wanted my son to feel valued and loved, to know that he could be himself—spiked hair and all.

Saint Francis of Assisi once said, "Preach the gospel at all times. If necessary, use words." I realized that day in my garage that I was being given an opportunity to preach the gospel without words to my son and his friends who stood by watching with grudging admiration. So I went after that hairdo with all the aplomb I could muster, and as I stood back to admire my handiwork at the end, I experienced in a profound way the depth of God's love for that child of mine.

Our privilege as followers of Christ is not only to carry his

> *Living so, with our hearts longing to have Jesus glorified in the souls He is seeking after, let us offer ourselves to Him for practical expressions of mercy. . . . There is work in a hundred different paths that the Spirit of Christ opens up through those who allow themselves to be led by Him.*
>
> Andrew Murray, *Abide in Me*

presence into every relationship but also to demonstrate his love through practical ways. How do we get to the point where this comes naturally to us, where we see people as Jesus does and relate to them as he would in any given situation? There is great power in the public proclamation of Christ's life and death and resurrection, but the truth is that, for a variety of reasons, many people aren't willing to listen. What will enable us to be conduits of the good news of Jesus Christ in the things we do as well as the words we speak?

First and foremost, we must experience the heart of Christ for ourselves, for we can give away only that which we have received. Spending time in the company of Jesus enables us to learn firsthand from the One who is gentle and humble in spirit, and as we do, we taste of the sweetness of his compassion for us as individuals and for the people he has placed within our sphere. When this happens, we begin to see their needs in an entirely different light, and it becomes almost second nature for us to practice acts of kindness, whether small or great. Without even realizing it, we find ourselves preaching the gospel without words.

Jesus described this as offering a cup of cold water in his name, promising that none who did so would lose their reward. I see in this promise two elements that can make a difference in how we approach this matter. First, he gives us the scope, which is that we do *all* in his name. We are Christ's ambassadors; we no longer live for ourselves, for he has bought us with a price and now our every action is his to direct. Whether he tells us to wash a neighbor's car or give a homeless person a cup of coffee or invite a visitor home from church or help a friend with her taxes, we do so as those who have tasted of his goodness and find our fulfillment in passing it along.

I saw this often as I was growing up. Our house seemed to have a revolving door, with everyone from total strangers to long-lost relatives coming and going. Mom could have written a book on how to stretch a single chicken to feed a crowd. We all love hearing the story of her waking early one morning to find two strange men sleeping on the floor in the living room. My brother had let them in and given them some blankets without even asking who they were—just doing what came naturally in our home. Though Mom and Dad modeled preaching the gospel without words, I often heard Dad tell those who thanked him, "You'll have to thank Jesus, because he's the one who changed my life." All that my parents did, they did in the name of Jesus.

The second element in Jesus' promise about a cup of water is that we should expect it to be rewarding, not only in eternity but also right now. A unique joy comes to us when we operate with Jesus' heart, pursuing his vision for other people. While the same good deeds might make us feel put out under other condi-tions, doing them with the sense that Jesus has called and being aware that he delights to use us for his purposes makes it a dif-ferent thing altogether.

There is a mystery and a wonder in experiencing the pleasure of God as we touch people in practical ways. To know that he sees, even if no one else does, that he looks upon us and smiles and says, "Well done," is the greatest reward we can have. God's pleasure is a strange and wonderful thing, a treasure we'll never lose. We can experience it right now and it will be ours in eter-nity when the storehouse of life episodes in which we have al-lowed Jesus to work through us will be opened up before his judgment seat.

Recently a friend and I had the privilege of cleaning for a

friend whose physical condition had made it impossible for her to do any housework for more than two years. Her husband, having overdosed on prescription painkillers a few weeks before, had left to try and get his life in order, and her hope was at an all-time low. We felt the oppression in that place when we arrived, a pall that hung in the air. So we cleaned. We filled our buckets and washed and sorted and dusted and moved furniture around and vacuumed until that place shone like a brand-new penny. As we worked, we sang and we prayed and we watched as the light of Christ began to fill that house. The peace and hope that settled in the atmosphere was almost palpable. We left there full of joy.

I awoke the next day sore and tired but with an amazing sense of Christ's love and tender care. The woman whose house we'd cleaned called to say that even her cats were dancing around the living room as if they knew something had changed. There was an honor in what we'd done that felt so pure, so fully good and right, that I could only shake my head in awe. I am convinced that the gospel went forth in power as we cleaned, glorifying the name of the King of kings and Lord of lords.

This is our high calling and joyful privilege—to be Christ to spiked-hair kids and deadbeat dads and lonely widows and unsuspecting neighbors and undeserving coworkers. Day in and day out, we offer a cup of water in Jesus' name—whatever that might mean—as we preach the gospel without words. And when we do, the axis upon which eternity sits shifts ever so slightly as angels dance at our Father's delight.

MAKING THE CHAOS SACRED

Join with your family or some friends in looking for opportunities to represent the gospel without words. Look especially for things you can do that no one except God will know you've done. Ask him to enable you to experience the joy and wonder of his pleasure as you go in his name.

A Vision for the World

After these things I looked, and behold, a great multitude
which no one could count, from every nation and all tribes and peoples
and tongues, standing before the throne and before the Lamb.

REVELATION 7:9

Teresa of Ávila, a fiery woman of God in sixteenth-century Spain, asked him to give her insight into what a soul saved by grace actually looked like. And then one night, as she was praying, she received a vision of a large crystal globe shaped like a castle with seven separate rooms, the one at the center being the most magnificent thing she'd ever seen. There she saw the King of glory seated on his throne, shining forth with a dazzling light that illuminated all the other rooms. Teresa never got over the wonder of that vision of God in her soul. Throughout her life, she longed for others to see what she'd seen, for she felt that once anybody grasped the beauty and splendor of such grace, they would never be the same.

Though I've never had the kind of experience Teresa had that night, I have been deeply impacted by a vision of Christ's throne as well, the one that the apostle John saw on the isle of Patmos

(Revelation 4). In that lonely place Jesus came to him, revealing a sight so astounding that John could only fall on his face. Drawn up into the scene, the aging disciple soon beheld the Lord, his throne encompassed by an emerald rainbow and radiating with glorious beams reflected from the sea of glass beneath his feet. Who can imagine what such a thing must have meant to that beloved saint so far from home?

As I've pondered that passage in prayer, I've been deeply changed in many ways, but one particular aspect of that scene has captivated me. Surrounding the throne of Christ, John saw a multitude of worshipers—so great a number that no one could count—from every nation and all tribes and peoples and tongues, all clothed in white robes and waving palm branches as they bowed before the King of kings (Revelation 7:9).

Have you ever wondered why God told John the end of the story? Why he had him write it down in such detail for us to read some two thousand years later? I believe in part it was because of his plan to involve you and me in the process of bringing it about. John saw the ending of a saga that day, one that was etched upon God's heart before the foundation of this world. The incredible reality is that he has made it possible for human beings to experience the joy of impacting the details of that narrative as it unfolds here on earth.

It reminds me of those books I read to my kids when they were little—the books where there were several possible story lines and we got to choose which way we wanted to go. If we turned to this page, the story would lead down one path; if we selected another, we'd be taken a different way altogether. But the end always turned out the same. The only thing that varied was the manner in which we got there.

That you and I can help to sculpt the landscape on the road we travel to that eternal destiny is mind boggling. Scripture says we are a vapor, that we're like grass that flourishes one day and is blown away by the wind the next. Yet from the moment the Almighty redeems us, he delights in using these earthen vessels to craft the course of that event toward which all of history is heading.

In any given week I receive e-mail updates from various people who live across the world, missionaries who are doing their part in this incredible plan. There was a time when I would read them and wish I was called to something as glorious as serving on some foreign field. But the more God's love for the nations has taken root in me, the greater my understanding that he intends to use me, and indeed every one of us, in ways that are no less important in the grand scheme of things. The key is in discovering what that might look like, given the current course of our lives. Now, for example, when I receive those newsletters, I spend a few minutes asking God to show me how to pray, often shooting off a quick e-mail to tell the writer what God has put on my heart for them.

Recently a couple who work in Sudan spoke at our church. I had followed their ministry and often felt overwhelmed at the conditions they lived in and the sacrifices they made, only to have their lives threatened, their belongings stolen and their hearts broken by the betrayal of nationals they had invested themselves in. I couldn't wait to hear firsthand from these heroes of the faith. Before the service, the wife pulled me aside to thank me for my e-mails, sharing how at times they'd been the one thing that kept her going. I was deeply touched. How incredible to think that something as simple as a prayer and an e-mail could play a part in the drama that is being inscribed on eternity's scrolls!

These are the kinds of privileges afforded each one of us who are called by Christ's name, and it matters not where we live or what our lifestyle entails. Indeed simply being aware and available can make the most mundane aspects of our lives pulse with purpose. For example, shopping, whether for clothes or groceries or furniture or cars, takes on a different hue when we remember that money is a means by which we can invest in eternity. Routine things, such as cleaning bathrooms or washing the car, become full of potential as we pray for missionaries in Jordan or Sudan or Belize or Bangladesh while scrubbing away. The point is that, because God has told us what the future holds and enabled us to join him in bringing it about, we can live each day with a sense of destiny that the rest of the world will never know.

> *All of history is moving toward one great goal, the white-hot worship of God and his Son among all the peoples of the earth.*
>
> John Piper, *Let the Nations be Glad*

The throne room vision John was given is the climax of God's story, the apex of human history. It is the moment for which God created the earth and called forth a people to be his own. And it is the purpose for which he sent his Son to die. This was the impetus behind Christ's final command to go into all the world and preach the gospel—that men and women and boys and girls from every tribe and tongue would one day see him face to face, be stunned by his beauty and fall down in awe as they give him the glory due his name.

For two thousand years Christ's followers have pursued that vision—some traveling far, while others the spread the news near home; some sharing his love with people who had never heard before, while others intercede on their behalf. Until he comes again, Jesus will continue to call us forth—some to stay and some to send and some to go and some to give. But for every single one of us, our quest and call, our privilege and purpose, our destiny and delight is to join the throng of saints who have gone before us in bringing others to bow before the King of kings and Lord of lords on that great and final day.

MAKING THE CHAOS SACRED

Over the next several days, focus on the throne room scene in Revelation 4. Read through a few verses at a time, using the principles of lectio divina and jotting down the things the Lord reveals to you. Throughout that day, look at your life and consider the ways God might want to involve you—in giving, going, praying or ministering to those who do. Seek to incorporate these actions over the next several months, making whatever practical changes you need to do so.

Seasons of the Soul

O God, You have taught me from my youth,
And I still declare Your wondrous deeds.
And even when I am old and gray, O God, do not forsake me,
Until I declare Your strength to this generation,
Your power to all who are to come.

PSALM 71:17-18

I don't know at what point I actually became a Christian. I realize that conventional wisdom (or at least my own upbringing) says that I should know, that I ought to be able provide the time, place and circumstances of my conversion on demand. But I simply can't. I walked the aisle when I was five, and got baptized then, mostly because it seemed the right thing to do. I did it again when I was sixteen in case that first time—which I could barely remember—didn't take, so to speak. And a few times along the road, I've "put a stake in the ground," as preachers are wont to advise us, to make sure I hadn't missed the boat. I think this is enough to certify me as a card-carrying, born-again evangelical.

Truth be told, I can never remember a time when I didn't love Jesus and want him in my life. I talked to him from my earliest years, loved all the stories about his life and was captivated by his death. My favorite hymn as a schoolgirl, "The Old Rugged Cross," was on page 93 in the *Baptist Hymnal*—a fact I knew well (much to the chagrin of our church music director, who tried to ignore my waving hand on Sunday evening hymn sings— but that's another story). The point of all this is simply to say that, as best I can tell, I've walked with the Lord for almost half a century now.

If I were to try to describe my journey in one pithy sentence, I'd borrow the title of that great Eugene Peterson book *A Long Obedience in the Same Direction,* which he borrowed from a German philosopher. Here's what I love about it.

For one thing, it reminds me that there are no shortcuts or easy answers for the condition of my sinful heart, only the day in and day out, sometimes exhilarating but more often tedious, work of maturing in Christ. When I was younger, I tended to get disheartened by this—weighed down by the thought of how far I had to go. But over the years, coming to terms with the fact that I'm in it for the long haul has made it easier for my spirit to peace-fully coexist with those areas of my still unsanctified soul.

The other thing about the phrase that I like is the part about going in the same direction, because it makes discipleship so simple, so attainable. Though there have been plenty of times when I felt as if I were going two steps forward and one step back, the truth is that for a very long time—for decades in fact—by the grace of God I've continued to move ahead.

Maybe the tendency to reminisce comes with age, but lately I've been thinking about what I wish I had done differently, given what I know now. Peterson says that this is a good thing to do, that our roots in the past can be a stabilizing force for today's obedience. I agree and hope as well that the things God has worked into my own heart might serve to encourage others along the way. To that end, join me as I meander a bit over some of the seasons of my own soul.

There was the season, for example, when my kids were young and life revolved around their needs. If I could go back, I would relieve the pressure that I put on myself to be so spiritual. Most of the new moms I talk with feel as I did, namely that they will never get it right, that their spiritual life has been shipwrecked on a sea of dirty diapers and late-night feedings. Not recognizing that this will pass all too quickly, we load ourselves down with guilt and fail to enjoy the incredible grace of having kids.

When our first son was born, I set myself up for a rude awakening by being determined not to lose any momentum in my spiritual growth. Barely able to find time to comb my hair, it was impossible to spend what felt like quality time with God. I remember reading a book about how "beautiful" Christian women could discipline themselves by getting up for an hour in the middle of the night for prayer, so I decided to try it. (Since I was sorely sleep deprived anyway, how could it get any worse?) I don't remember how long that fiasco lasted, but I do recall bribing myself with a bowl of ice cream in order to get out of bed a night or two. In looking back, I'm pretty sure all I gained was a few unwanted pounds.

By the time our second son came along ten years later, I was a little wiser and felt a whole lot older, and I knew that at best I'd be connecting with God in hit-and-miss fashion, grabbing whatever opportunities for prayer might pop up during the course of a day. What surprised me was how easy this was once I gave myself permission to think in a fresh way. I did things like read

Scripture aloud while feeding my baby and worship while I sang him to sleep at night. As he got older, instead of feeling cheated or irritated when he came bouncing in just as I'd settled down for morning devotions, I would welcome him to join me, short attention span and all. Now that he is nineteen, my son demands hardly any time from me and certainly never interrupts me in the early morning hours. But those days when I got to sing and read to him as a baby, or hold his head on my lap as a toddler while I prayed, are precious memories I wouldn't trade for anything in the world.

Something else I'd handle differently are the seasons I spent in the wilderness. I know everyone has them—those weeks or months when God's Word becomes dry, ministry feels burdensome and prayer seems like an exercise in futility. Having wandered there on a number of occasions, I understand now that when God seems furthest from me,

> *We are most deeply asleep at the switch when we fancy we control any switches at all. We sleep to time's hurdy-gurdy; we wake, if we ever wake, to the silence of God.*
>
> **Annie Dillard, in *Pilgrim Souls***

he is accomplishing the most in strengthening my faith and maturing my love for him. Though I wouldn't change *what* I did during the dryness (I'd still try to read Scripture and pray and fellowship with others), I would have reminded myself more often that though I couldn't see or feel him, God was escorting me every step of the way and in his faithfulness he'd make sure I got through to the other side. Having that perspective would have freed me from a lot of pointless striving and perhaps enabled me to enjoy more of what the Lord had for me in the journey.

On the flip side of the coin, I would try to remember never to take those glorious seasons of Christ's tangible presence lightly, realizing that they too come and go. I would savor the moments when my time with Jesus felt sweet and be more in awe of experiences in worship that brought me so close to heaven that I felt I could almost touch his holiness. I would write all that I'd seen with my spiritual eyes in a journal and record any words I heard the Lord speaking, keeping a detailed account of the revelations he gave me from his Word.

These things I would do, knowing that a season of darkness—moments or hours or months when nothing would make sense, when the voice of God would be entirely silent and his presence a distant dream—might await me. Then, when that dark night of my soul came, I would have something to return to, a track record of God's dealings that might sustain me and give me faith until I could behold his face once again.

There are many other things I'd probably do differently, but if I could narrow it down to one thing, it would be to relax and try to glean from the here and now, knowing that God is always at work, no matter how things appear to me. I would remember that in his sovereign wisdom God personally directs the course of my life, determining what I need to learn and how I can best experience growth. I would embrace the process with less pressure and more peace, knowing that God, who saved me through no merit of my own, is more passionate about sanctifying me than I ever will be. Because I have seen how much he loves his glory, I would rest in his plan to make me a bearer of it, ever confident that he who began a good work in me will be faithful to complete it until the day of Christ Jesus (Philippians 1:6).

I find great comfort in knowing that my days are written in

God's eternal book—I cannot add to them or take even one away. But when he does come for me, I want to meet him with a spring in my step and a song on my lips and the kind of delight in my heart that affirms that every minute has been worth it. Until then I'm going to continue this long obedience in the same direction. I'm looking forward to the mountains God will yet call me to climb, the oceans whose depths he'll bid me plumb, the valleys into which I'll inevitably descend and all the other seasons of my soul that he will transform into something sacred for his glory and for my joy.

MAKING THE CHAOS SACRED

What are some seasons you've experienced in your spiritual journey? Take time to think prayerfully about these, jotting down what you wish you had done differently and what you've gleaned through the ups and downs. Offer praise to God for his faithfulness to you through it all. Commit to sharing what you've seen with a spouse or friend or your small group.

Extended Experiments in Prayer

A Thirty-Minute Experiment in Prayer

Thirty minutes is ample time to connect with God in meaningful ways. Plan when this will best work for you and prepare ahead by having your Bible, a journal and a pen ready to go. Also, choose a spot where you will be free from interruptions.

SETTLING YOUR SOUL

5–10 minutes

- Breathe slowly and deeply, acknowledging that God is with you. Sometimes it is good to speak out loud, saying something like "God, you are here with me. You are here in me. You are here all around me. I embrace your presence." Speak the name of Jesus and let the joy of being his child settle upon you.

- Release distractions by offering them one by one to the Lord. Cast any burdens on him, knowing that he cares about all of it. Have a piece of paper nearby so that you can jot down things that you need to take care of later. Gently bring your mind back to the Lord each time it wanders, thanking him again that he is present with you.

- Take some time to let yourself experience how you are really feeling. What is going on inside you? How do you feel about this time with the Lord? Restless? Sleepy? Fearful? Anxious? Excited? Share your feelings freely with God.

- Ask the Lord if there is anything that might keep you from experiencing and enjoying his presence during this time. Confess any sins he might reveal and bask in his full forgiveness.

- Resist the devil and he will flee. Identify and renounce any lies Satan may be throwing your way (things like "You don't deserve to be here," "You'll never last thirty minutes," "You're going to fail," "God doesn't care about intimacy with you" and so on).

LECTIO—LISTENING/READING

5–10 minutes

Choose a passage for this time, or if you prefer, select one from the following list: Romans 12:1-2; 2 Corinthians 2:14-16; Ephesians 1:18-23; Hebrews 1:3.

- Read the verse or passage slowly a couple of times, if possible aloud at least once.

- Read it again, mulling it over in your mind and letting the words sink in.

- Read it one more time, stopping when a key idea or significant thought touches you. Wait in silence for God.

MEDITATIO—MEDITATION

5–10 minutes

- Read the passage again slowly. Ask, "Lord, what are you saying to me?"

- Wait quietly for the Lord to speak to your heart. What does he want you personally to understand?
- When he speaks, turn it over in your mind, musing on what you feel is the heart of his word to you.
- Write down what you sense him saying.

ORATIO—PRAYER

5–10 minutes

- Consecrate yourself to the Lord, who wants to engage in loving conversation with you. Tell him what you have seen or understood thus far.
- Wait for God to show you how this truth might change your perspective, your way of life, the way you treat others or your relationship with him and so forth. Ask, "Lord, what would you have me do?"
- Jot down at least one thing that you will do differently today as a result of what you believe you had heard from God.

CONTEMPLATIO—CONTEMPLATION

5–10 minutes

- Rest in God's presence. See yourself in his embrace. Receive his love, not for something you have done, but simply because he loves you.
- Practice loving him back in silence. Any time you start to feel restless, fix your gaze upon him by slowly speaking some form of his name or a description of his character (Jesus, Savior, Messiah, Lord, King, Living Water, Bread of Life, Good Shepherd, Counselor and so on) a few times softly, gently and worshipfully.

- Converse with Christ as you desire, but return to quiet adoration as much as possible.

- As you move from here, continue to practice God's presence, which is as real wherever you go today as it has been in your waiting and listening through focused prayer.

A One-Hour Experiment in Prayer

Spending an hour with God can be one of life's greatest pleasures. Plan ahead for this time by setting aside the hour, perhaps on some weekend morning or a lengthy lunch break from work or an evening when you have no other commitments.

Collect needed items, such as your Bible, a journal and a pen, and prepare the area you will spend the time in, possibly by lighting candles and playing soft instrumental music. Plan this in the same way you might plan for a date, anticipating the great time you are going to have and the things you will glean from the heart of God. You may be surprised at how quickly the time goes and may want to schedule another one as soon as possible.

Looking Up

Approximately 10 minutes

- Breathe deeply for a few moments. Each time you inhale, picture the things you want to take into your heart—God's love, faithfulness, grace, goodness and so on. With each exhale, release things that hinder you—sins, fears, doubts, distractions. Sometimes it is helpful to do this out loud. For example, while inhaling, you could say, "Lord, I receive your peace." While exhaling, you could say, "Lord, I release anxiety and stress." (If you're in a public place, do this under your breath.)

- Read one of the psalms of ascent (Psalms 120−134), aloud if possible. Wait quietly as you consider the God who is beyond our limited knowledge. See him exalted above the heavens and enthroned within your heart. Do not rush past this time. Let these truths wash over you.

LOOKING WITHIN

Approximately 10 minutes

This is a time for the prayer of examen, a time to give thanks, to wait upon God and to allow his Spirit to prepare your heart to receive all he has for you.

- Speak gently to the Lord, affirming that he is not a distant God but is present with you in every way, right now, right here.

- As you look back at the past day, ponder the events and the places where God was at work. Give thanks for each one.

- Seek the illumination of God's Spirit, asking him to show you what you need to see for this particular time.

- Look back over the past day prayerfully and consider: What attitudes of my heart have been unhealthy? What harmful actions have I taken? Are there people I have slighted or failed to love as Christ does? Confess these things, receiving God's full forgiveness.

LOOKING TO GOD'S WORD

Approximately 30 minutes

- Open your Bible to the Sermon on the Mount, which begins at Matthew 5:1. Ask the Holy Spirit to guide you as you read.

- Slowly begin to read until you feel a gentle nudge in your spirit directing you to a particular teaching in the sermon (it might be one verse or it might be several). Wait in quietness for a moment and then read that portion of the sermon again, asking the Holy Spirit to speak personally and directly to you from it. Let the words wash over you.

- Prayerfully complete this thought: "Lord, what I see about you here is . . ." If you desire, write this out in your journal.

- Now slowly and prayerfully read the same words you just read, acknowledging God's presence and tender compassion for you and others. Give yourself time to feel his embrace, then complete this thought: "Lord, what I see about myself and others here is . . ." If you desire, write this out in your journal.

- Read the same words one more time. Ponder them in light of your life right now and think about how they might apply to situations you are facing. Prayerfully complete this thought: "Lord, what I believe you are calling me to do in light of these words is . . ." If you desire, write this out in your journal.

- If there is time left and you want to continue, read on in the passage until the Holy Spirit nudges you toward another teaching, then go through the same questions.

LOOKING OUT

Approximately 10 minutes

- Look ahead, quietly viewing the path you will be taking in the coming hours or days. Consider the appointments you have, the people you will be involved with, the goals you want to achieve and so forth. Offer yourself to the Lord, asking him for grace to reflect Christ's presence in all you do.

- Rest quietly in the Lord as you see him moving before you into the busyness of your day. Follow him.

A Three-Hour Experiment in Prayer

Getting away from the hustle and bustle of life to spend an entire morning or afternoon or evening with the Lord is not easy to do, but it is well worth the effort. The format I am offering here enables you to look back and also look to the future, as you seek to hear God's voice and learn what he desires for this season of your life. Of course you'll need to plan ahead by canceling appointments. If you have the time, you might want to spread this exercise out over an entire day, but it can be done in three hours.

I also recommend, if possible, that you get away from your home or workplace, as the needs there tend to be distracting. Not sure where to go? Let me help with some tips.

- Many retreat centers offer their facilities for day use for free or for a nominal fee.
- Swap houses with a friend for the time frame, then get together with the friend and share how it went.
- Go to a local park or beach.
- Find a quiet nook in a community library.
- Divide the time between places. You might, for example, begin at a local library and then head to a park or the beach, then to a coffee shop.

You will need your Bible (you may want a couple of versions), a journal and a pen. If it is feasible, you might also want to bring some music (instrumental and worship) and something on which to play it.

HOUR ONE: REFLECTION

In this first hour, you will be looking back, allowing God to refresh and renew you. Then you will take some time to receive his love through contemplation.

To begin, thank God for his presence with you here. Read Psalm 9:1 aloud as praise to him. Make a thanksgiving list and a praise list. In the thanksgiving list, write ten specific ways God has blessed your life. In the praise list, write ten specific things about him that are praiseworthy. Offer these in worship to the Lord.

Read Hebrews 3:12-19 slowly and prayerfully. Be still as you consider the verses you have read. Ask the Holy Spirit to speak to your heart and read the passage again. Now, as you seek God's face, complete this sentence: "Lord, over the past several days I have struggled to find rest in . . ." (This might involve circumstances at work, home, church or school, relationships with family, friends, neighbors or fellow believers, finances, time commitments and the like.) Write each one down with one summary statement about the nature of the struggle.

Read Hebrews 3:12-19 again. Ask the Holy Spirit to speak to you once more and then complete this sentence: "Lord, I sometimes fail to believe You are really working in . . ." Write down whatever he reveals.

Repent for your unbelief and receive God's full forgiveness. Read Proverbs 3:5-6. Let these truths wash over each situation you mentioned above, exposing any lies and renouncing them before God.

Sit quietly for a few moments, enjoying God's rest.

Ask the Lord for the grace to love him in quietness and to receive his love in response. Read Psalm 123:1-2 two or three times silently. Look with spiritual eyes at God by focusing on the truth that he is all sufficient, everything you need. Stay in a state of silent adoration for a few minutes, savoring the wonder of a

God who walks in gentleness before you, always showing you the way. Offer the words "Whom have I in heaven but You? And besides You, I desire nothing on earth" (Psalm 73:25) whenever your mind wanders or you feel antsy.

As you share your love with the Lord, receive his love for you. Picture him singing over you, rejoicing over you, delighting in the unique reflection of his Son that he sees in your soul. Write a prayer of thanksgiving, affirming that the love God gives you can never be taken away.

End this hour by taking a break. You may want to go for a short walk or do a few gentle physical exercises and stretches. Get a drink, have a snack, move around and relax for ten minutes. (If you are using three different locations, this is the time for your first switch.)

HOUR TWO: PETITION

This hour will include a guided exercise in two parts: supplication for your own needs and intercession for the needs of others.

Supplication: prayer on your own behalf. Take some time once again to acknowledge God's presence with you and his purpose for this time. Read Paul's words in Romans 11:36 (aloud if possible) a few times.

Ponder the reality that all that you have—even the air you breathe this moment—is a gift from your Father. Acknowledge the truth of this by taking a deep breath and thanking him that you are alive because he gave you that breath.

Prayerfully consider the personal needs you face right now—physical, spiritual or emotional. Which are the most urgent for you? Which ones weigh the heaviest on your heart and mind? Make a list of these in your journal.

See yourself as a needy child sitting with your caring Father. Read each need and ask him to care for you by meeting this need. Place your hands open on your lap in a posture of receiving and picture God moving to meet that need. Listen for his voice. If he speaks to you about this need or how he wants to meet it, write it down.

Remembering that his ways of answering may be far different from what you expect, release your expectations to the Lord and thank him that you can rest in him.

Intercession: prayer on behalf of others. God loves intercession—it is like a sweet-smelling aroma wafting to his throne. As you sit before him, picture the prayers you will be offering ascending to him, delighting his heart.

Consider another believer for whom you might spend some time in prayer. It could be one of your children, a brother or sister, a pastor, a missionary, a Sunday school teacher or a Bible study leader. This person might be a mature Christian, a new believer or even someone living outside God's will right now. Ask God to place one person on your heart.

Thank the Holy Spirit for the promise that he will work in and through you, praying God's will for this person.

Read Paul's prayer in Ephesians 1:18-20. Take some time to offer up each phrase of this prayer in your own words on behalf of the person for whom you are interceding. As you finish each phrase, pause and wait on the Lord, asking him to reveal specific things to pray for the person. In your journal, write down anything he shows you.

When you are finished, spend a few minutes offering prayers of faith—thanking God for what he has promised to do. Rejoice that your confidence isn't in your ability to pray in the right way but in God's passion for his own glory and his determination to work in the lives of his beloved.

End this hour by taking a break for ten to fifteen minutes. Lie down and listen to quiet instrumental music if possible. Close your eyes and try to rest without falling asleep. If you do find yourself waking up from a sleep, however, remember that you are in the arms of the Lord and that there is no condemnation there. In addition, you probably really needed that physical break. (If you are changing locations, this is the second switch.)

HOUR THREE: A TIME TO LOOK AHEAD

Welcome God to this final hour of your special time with him. You will be finishing your time by looking at the weeks to come, seeking to gain God's perspective so that you can go from here with a sense of joyful anticipation of what the future holds.

Make a list of the key components of your life at this time. These might include family, work, leisure, physical health, church, ministry, friendships and others. Bring each thing before the Lord, considering the plans you may already have made or may need to make for the coming days. Then ask God to speak in response to these questions:

- "Lord, what do you want to say to me about Your desire for this area of my life?"
- "Lord, is there any specific guidance You want to give me concerning this area of my life in the coming weeks?"

Make sure to write what you sense God saying for each thing in your journal. When you have finished, make a list of specific action steps you might take to follow through on what God has shown you.

Spend whatever time is left of this final hour by thanking and praising God for his goodness to you. Make plans now for another three-hour meeting with God in a few months.

A One-Day Experiment in Prayer
as a Community

Some of the most meaningful times of experiencing God's presence can be found in community. This exercise (designed to last approximately eight hours, plus some leeway time to arrive and get settled) can be a mini retreat for a group of any size. There are five sessions—three for the group and two for individuals, plus a break for lunch and rest. For groups who prefer to make this into a retreat, the sections can be spread out over two days instead, allowing more time for each one.

Location. The group will need a leader who plans ahead by securing a location that provides a group setting as well as areas where individuals can be alone. Many retreat centers offer day rates for this kind of thing. The group could also meet at a church building or in someone's home, or if weather and space permit, at an outdoor area such as a park or beach.

Supplies. Each person will need to bring his or her Bible, a journal and a pen. The facilitator should also bring a contemporary version of Scripture such as The Message or the New Living Translation. If he or she does not own one, these versions can be found online and it will be helpful to print out a modern version of each passage that will be used (see www.biblegateway.com, for example).

Meals. Ideally the time together will begin after breakfast. Each person can bring a sack lunch so that the group does not have to spend a lot of time in preparation of food. If time permits, the group can plan to go out to dinner or fix a meal together at the end of the retreat. (Some retreat centers also provide meals for a minimal price.)

Preparation. It is helpful for all participants to read through the exercise ahead of time. The leader also needs to be well acquainted with the format.

SESSION ONE: GROUP LECTIO DIVINA (MATTHEW 5:38-48)

One hour

The first hour will be a group exercise focusing on Matthew 5:38-48 in which participants listen as the passage is read aloud four times (twice in the first section, then once each time following), sharing specific responses. The leader should be prepared to briefly explain this to the group and then assign the four readers, making sure the final reader has a modern version to use.

Begin by taking time to quiet hearts and welcome God's presence. Offer up sentence prayers of praise and thanksgiving.

First reading. In this reading each participant will be asking the Holy Spirit to reveal some specific truth about who God is, what his character is like, how he works and so on. Follow this format:

- Two people take turns reading the passage aloud slowly and meditatively.

- Participants wait in silence, praying and pondering what they have heard and what phrase, thought or word about God resonates from it.

- Each group member then briefly shares the truth about God that has spoken to him or her, without teaching or expounding. (It is important that participants share briefly, to keep the focus on the Scripture. After the final reading, they will have time to share in greater detail.)

- *Second reading.* In this reading participants will be asking the

Holy Spirit to speak to them about how God relates to them
and to the world in light of this passage.

- One person reads the passage aloud slowly.
- The group waits again in silence as they pray and consider the
  words, asking God to speak.
- Participants share what they have heard God speaking by
  making brief statements starting with "I hear . . ." or "I see . . ."
  Once again, they should not explain or expound.

Third reading. In this reading, participants will seek to hear
any specific actions God would have them take in response to
what they have heard.

- One person reads the passage aloud, this time from a contemporary version such as The Message.
- In silence group members take time to reflect on the question
  "God, what do you want me to do, to see or to be today in response to this passage?"
- Participants share what they have heard and gained from their
  reflection on the passage and what they would like prayer for
  in response. This time of sharing will be a little longer than the
  previous two times.

Ending prayer. Participants then pray for each other, based on
what has been shared. The group may divide into pairs, or if the
group is small, each person can pray aloud for the person on his
or her right. The facilitator will end the time of prayer and dismiss the group for individual time during the next hour.

SESSION TWO: INDIVIDUAL REFLECTING ON GOD'S FAITHFULNESS
One-and-a-half hours

Spend a few minutes quieting your own heart. Looking back over your spiritual journey, make a list of key seasons, events and experiences that have shaped your relationship with God. You can work from the present backward or begin with your earliest spiritual memories and work forward. After you've listed these things, try to depict your life in Christ thus far by drawing a road with signposts along the way showing what has taken place. Be sure to show sharp turns, detours, dead ends, ups and downs and so on.

When you are finished, ask God to help you pinpoint at least three specific ways you have been shaped by the way your journey has taken place. Write them down.

As you look back at God's faithful hand, take some time to give him thanks. Read Romans 8:28-29 and Psalm 138:8. Worship him for the ways in which he has worked all things together for good in your life, accomplishing his purposes in and through you.

SESSION THREE: GROUP SHARING AND PRAYER

One hour

During this hour the group will meet together and share. Since there is most likely not time for each to share his or her entire journey (unless the group is very small), each person can share one or two highlights and then the three ways the person has been shaped through it. After each participant has shared, the group may offer prayers of praise and thanksgiving, if time allows. The leader then can dismiss the group to lunch and rest time.

LUNCH AND REST

One hour

For the next hour the group will eat together and take a time of rest. Participants should seek to maintain an attitude of awareness that God is present and working even in the fellowship of a meal together. Avoid discussions about external issues or other people and seek to commune over what God is doing through this time and in your lives right now. After lunch, participants may talk a walk, lie down for a nap or simply close their eyes and listen to soothing worship music. When the hour is up, the leader should call the group back together.

SESSION FOUR: LECTIO DIVINA (MATTHEW 7:1-12)

One hour

Using the same format as session one, the group will now pray through this passage and share based on it. When they are finished, the leader should explain that participants will now be spending two hours alone with the Lord. This will be a time of silence in which group members will not speak to each other until the two hours are complete.

SESSION FIVE: INDIVIDUAL RECEIVING GOD'S PURPOSES

Two hours

In this session you will be looking at your spiritual journey in the present and the future. The exercise about the future is longer than the one about the present, so plan accordingly. Begin by acknowledging God's presence with you during this session. Spend a few minutes thanking him specifically for all that he has already done today. Ask him to guide this time.

Now consider your spiritual life and the season you find yourself in right now. What does it look like? What encourages you? In what ways do you feel stuck? Describe your current stage in the journey in one of two ways: either write a short letter to some imaginary friend who hasn't seen you in a few years and tell this person about what you see God doing in you right now, or else draw a picture that symbolizes how you see your spiritual experience.

When you are finished, read Philippians 2:12-13. On one page, make two columns.

- In the first column, write down the ways in which you can affirm that God is at work within you right now. Thank him for the grace he has given to enable you to grow in him thus far.

- In the second column, write down the ways you feel you need to do more to work out your salvation. Ask the Holy Spirit for revelation. Offer the things he shows you to the Lord, trusting in his grace to enable you to go deeper in your commitment to him.

If you need to, take a break and walk around or listen to music before going to the next part.

In this second part you are going to establish a prayer plan for the coming weeks or months, using the prayer Jesus gave us as your example. First, read through the model prayer in Matthew 6:9-13 and Luke 11:2-4. Now divide the prayer into three categories, spending some time seeking the Lord over each one.

- Christ's reign ("Your kingdom come. Your will be done on earth, as it is in heaven"). Make a list of the key people and situations in your life right now. Ask the Lord these questions about each one: "Lord, what would your lordship look like here?" and "Lord, what is your will for this situation or person right now?" Jot down what you hear.

- Personal needs ("Give us this day our daily bread"). Consider your physical, spiritual, emotional and relational needs right now. Hear Jesus asking you this question: "What do you need? What can I do for you?" Jot down your responses to him.

- Spiritual warfare ("Forgive us our debts. . . . Do not lead us into temptation, but deliver us from evil"). First, ask God to reveal any unforgiveness you might have toward other people. Confess this as you release them from any debt you feel they have owed you and then receive God's forgiveness. Next, ask the Holy Spirit to reveal what your greatest areas of temptation are going to be in the coming days or weeks. Jot these down. Finally, ask the Holy Spirit to reveal what lies of Satan (unbelief, fear, offense, discouragement or whatever) you will need God to deliver you from. Write these down.

On a fresh piece of paper, write across the top: "Hallowed be your name." Then, based on what God has revealed to you, write the things you want to be praying for over the coming days. Consider what would be the easiest way for you to remember these in order to lift them up on a regular basis. Don't forget to list the specific things you will be asking God to do, based on what he has revealed during this time.

Across the bottom of the final page, write, "Yours is the kingdom and the power and the glory forever. Amen." Spend a few minutes praising God for hearing and answering prayer and for all he is going to do. Keep this page in your Bible so you can refer back to it in prayer often.

SESSION SIX: GROUP SHARING AND PRAYER

One hour

The group will now come back together to share some of the things God showed them during their personal prayer time. Participants will first share their letter or picture of their spiritual journey as it is at present. Then, if there is time, group members can share some of the things they will be praying for in the future based on what God revealed to them.

The group then should end the day with a time of thanksgiving, praise and worship for all God has done.

Attributes of God with Scriptures

Holiness	1 Samuel 2:2; Psalm 77:13
Mercy	Daniel 9:9; Hebrews 2:17
Righteousness	Ezra 9:15; Psalm 145:17
Goodness	Jeremiah 33:11; John 10:14
Faithfulness	Psalm 91:4; Isaiah 25:1
Justice	Job 34:12; Psalm 89:14
Love	Ephesians 3:16-19
Omnipotence	2 Chronicles 20:6; Romans 1:20
Omniscience	Proverbs 15:3; Hebrews 4:13
Omnipresence	Jeremiah 23:23-24; Psalm 139:7-10

Descriptions of Jesus with Scriptures

Creator	John 1:3; Colossians 1:16
Resurrection	John 11:25-26; Philippians 1:21
Power of God	Romans 1:16; Luke 22:69
Redeemer	Job 19:25-27; Isaiah 44:24; 1 Corinthians 6:20
King of kings	Psalm 145:10-13; Revelation 19:15-16
Light	John 1:9; Revelation 21:23-24
Teacher	Luke 6:40; John 13:13
Wisdom	1 Corinthians 1:24; Romans 11:33
Hope of glory	Colossians 1:27; Titus 2:13
Deliverer	Luke 4:18; Galatians 1:3-4
I Am	John 8:58; Revelation 22:13
Bread of Life	Psalm 22:26; John 6:35

Notes

Chapter 1: The Quiet Time Fixation

page 17   my favorite online Bible program: Bible Gateway <www.bible gateway.com> is a free online search engine with multiple translations available. I like it best for a quick and simple concordance. When I want to do more in-depth study, I use Study Light <www.studylight.org> or Blue Letter Bible <www.blueletterbible.org>, both of which include a number of commentaries, dictionaries and Strong's concordance with Greek and Hebrew word meanings for King James and New American Standard versions.

Chapter 2: Redefining Prayer

page 23   Survey: Ron Sellers, "Most Pastors Unsatisfied with Their Personal Prayer Lives" <http://lifeway.com/lwc/article_main_page>.

page 26   Some people practice daily office: An excellent resource for practicing the daily office is Phyllis Tickle, *The Divine Hours* (New York: Oxford University Press, 2007).

Chapter 4: As Simple as Turning

page 37   Anne Rice's *Christ the Lord:* Rice includes an afterword in the book that tells of her journey back to faith in Christ. For a detailed interview about this, see "Interview with a Penitent," *Christianity Today,* December 2005, p. 19. For further reading about Rice´s book, see <Beliefnet.com/story/

178/story_17806_1.html> and <benwitherington.blogspot
.com/search?q=anne+rice>.

Chapter 8: Seize the Silence

page 63   Mother Teresa once said: These words are taken from a
heartfelt letter that Mother Teresa wrote in her final years
to all who worked with the Missionaries of Charity. Though
much has been written since her death concerning her
lengthy dark night of the soul, this does not diminish the reality of the intimate, personal communion she had experienced with Christ. The entire letter is published in *Works
of Love Are Works of Peace,* a photographic record by
Michael Collopy (San Francisco: Ignatius Press, 1996), p.
197.

Chapter 11: A Life Small in His Hands

page 80   "Your efforts have been": Thomas C. Upham, *The Life of
Madame Guyon* (Augusta, Maine: Christian Books, 1984),
pp. 35-36.

Chapter 12: Getting Soaked on the Sabbath

page 92   Try altering the speed: See <http://www.embody.co.uk/
archive/safe/experiential/prayer11.html> for a fuller expla-
nation and other ideas.

Chapter 16: Unholy Moments

page 115   a nineteenth-century Russian pilgrim: The book *The Way
of the Pilgrim* and its sequel, *The Pilgrim Continues His
Way,* are still in print today and available from several pub-
lishers.

Chapter 17: The Heavens Declare

page 122   "appointed consummation": C. S. Lewis, *Reflections on the
Psalms* (New York: Harcourt, Brace & World, 1958), p. 95.

Chapter 18: Immersed *in* a World I'm Not *Of*

page 125 "as you continue on your journey": StudyLight.org New Testament Greek Lexicon, s.v. *poreuomai.* Accessed online at <http://www.studylight.org/lex/grk/view.cgi?number=4198>.

Chapter 22: Seasons of the Soul

page 152 If I were to try: Eugene Peterson, *A Long Obedience in the Same Direction* (Downers Grove, Ill.: InterVarsity Press, 2000), p. 16.

2110 ⑥
8/15 ⑬ 12/14